Slaying
Leviathan

RELATED TITLES FROM POTOMAC BOOKS

*The Cure for Our Broken Political Process: How We Can Get
Our Politicians to Resolve the Issues Tearing Our Country Apart*
— Sol Erdman and Lawrence Susskind

*The Mythology of American Politics: A Critical Response
to Fundamental Questions*
— John T. Bookman

Counting Every Vote: The Most Contentious Elections in American History
— Robert Dudley and Eric Shiraev

Slaying Leviathan

THE MORAL CASE FOR TAX REFORM

LESLIE CARBONE

Potomac Books, Inc.
Washington, D.C.

Library of Congress Cataloging-in-Publication Data
Carbone, Leslie.
  Slaying leviathan : the moral case for tax reform / Leslie Carbone. — 1st ed.
      p. cm.
  Includes bibliographical references.
  ISBN 978-1-59797-417-2 (hbk. : alk. paper)
  1. Fiscal policy—United States. 2. Taxation—United States—History. I. Title.
  HJ257.3.C37 2009
  336.2′050973—dc22

                                                            2009020758

Printed in the United States of America on acid-free paper that meets the American National Standards Institute Z39-48 Standard.

Potomac Books, Inc.
22841 Quicksilver Drive
Dulles, Virginia 20166

First Edition

10 9 8 7 6 5 4 3 2 1

In Memoriam

Mary Jane Homan

CONTENTS

ACKNOWLEDGMENTS

"It started with a mouse," said Walt Disney of what has become the world's most famous entertainment conglomerate.

This book started as a policy paper on the moral impact of tax policy; then it grew into a pamphlet. But as I researched the subject, it became clear that the study required book-length investigation.

Many of the ideas in this work were refined while I was at Family Research Council. I am grateful to many at FRC who helped shape my thoughts and my words, including Tom Atwood, Chuck Donovan, Bob Morrison, Bob Patterson, Susan Orr, Bill Mattox, Geri Harper, Vashti Pearson, Anna Ryan, Jennifer Wotochek, David Crowell, Whitney Rhoades, Charissa Kersten, Esther Kay, and Robert Preston.

The Heritage Foundation has been greatly helpful, hosting two roundtables to help me clarify the ideas in this work. For their help, I am indebted to: Adam Meyerson, Bill Beach, Matt Spalding, Dan Mitchell, Pat Fagan, Bruce Bartlett, Steve Slivinski, and James Anderson.

Many others from around the country have helped with this work as well. David Theroux read an early draft and has consistently provided much-needed encouragement and belief in this work. The late Jack Kemp, Burt Folsom, Bill Shughart, Eli Lehrer, and Ed Hudgins read drafts and provided thoughtful comments and encouraging words. Pete Sepp helped articulate the need for this work. Joe Lehman and the late Joe Overton provided strategic counsel. Grover Norquist allowed me to introduce the work at his weekly center-right coalition meeting.

Finally, Bryan Atchison has been a true friend and companion throughout the years of labor on this book.

INTRODUCTION

At 8:28 on a crisp Tuesday morning in September, as office workers were greeting each other around coffee machines, homemakers were clearing breakfast tables, and schoolchildren were opening their primers, Mohammed Atta and his gang of four other terrorists broke into the cockpit of American Airlines Flight 11. Brandishing knives and box-cutters, the five easily hijacked the plane, which carried eighty-seven other passengers and 10,000 gallons of fuel. Eighteen minutes later, Atta slammed the aircraft between the 94th and 99th floors of the World Trade Center's 110-story North Tower.

Seventeen minutes later, at 9:03, the tranquility of an ordinary morning shattered, horrified Americans watched as United Airlines Flight 175 crashed into the South Tower, between the 78th and 84th floors. Forty minutes later, at 9:43, American Airlines Flight 77 hit the west side of the Pentagon. At 10:09, the South Tower collapsed; one minute later, the damaged section of the Pentagon fell; at 10:28, the North Tower crumbled. Meanwhile, at 10:06, thanks to the heroic efforts of passengers on board, United Airlines Flight 93 crashed, not into another major national landmark, but into a Pennsylvania field.

What drove Mohammed Atta and eighteen others to destroy themselves in the worst terrorist attack on America's homeland in history? The answer, it appears, is resentment.

According to a report in the *International Herald Tribune,*

Atta's path, pieced together from interviews with people who knew him across 33 years and three continents, was a quiet and methodical evolution of resentment that . . . took a leap to mass-murderous fury.

Atta came of age in an Egypt torn between growing Western influence and the religious fundamentalism that gathered force in reaction. . . . [Once] on his own, in the West . . . his religious faith deepened and his resentments hardened. The focus of his disappointment became the Egyptian government; the target of his blame became the West, and especially America.[1]

Experts explain that many Middle Easterners labor under a deep resentment that the Arab world has lost dignity and is not the geopolitical player it feels entitled to be. Says John Esposito, director of the Center for Muslim-Christian Understanding at Georgetown University, "[T]hey feel impotent. The West, they feel, looks at them as backward and is only interested in their oil. Their sense of self-worth and identity is wounded."[2]

Atta particularly bemoaned Western influence in Arab cities—specifically, the rise of skyscrapers like those he ultimately destroyed. Absent from long stretches of coursework at the Technical University of Hamburg-Harburg, Atta explained that he was writing his master's thesis on the conflict between Islam and modernity as reflected in the planning of the city of Aleppo in northwestern Syria. Volker Hauth, a friend of Atta's who accompanied him on trips to Syria, told the *Los Angeles Times*, "I knew Mohammed as a guy searching for justice. . . . He felt offended by this broad wrong direction that the world was taking."[3]

Atta believed that he was justified in damaging the centers of the prosperity that has raised living standards the world over and even provided his own education. Atta's case was extreme, but the moralizing-wrapped resentment that drove him to destroy himself and others in the name of justice, the failure to look inward for the sources of problems, and the lack of understanding that greatness cannot be achieved by tearing others down plagues every human heart and frequently finds its object in the economic success of others.

Atta claimed to value justice, as do many who target the fruits of others' achievement, but it is a perverse understanding of justice that allows for destroying what another has built. What leads in the Middle East to terrorism leads in the West to discriminatory law against the objects of resentment. While terrorism destroyed the towers that symbolize economic power, discriminatory fiscal policy targets the wealth like that the towers housed. Just as Atta destroyed himself, those who sponsor resentment-based tax policies damage themselves and all society, both economically and morally. This moral dimension of tax policy has often been overlooked.

In a republican society, seemingly large fortunes make easy targets. While the hard work, risk-taking, and discipline required to create them often go unnoticed, the fortunes themselves provoke great interest. Estate homes offer tours to middle-class travelers; magazines feature glowing articles and glossy photographs extolling the priceless possessions, lavish parties, and rare license of the privileged class. A popular television series glorified the *Lifestyles of the Rich and Famous*. It requires no gift of uncommon insight to grasp how such exaltation would provoke resentment among the less privileged. Regrettably, rarer is the recognition that such resentment is corrosive to the individual whose character is marred by it, and not the sort of thing that public policy should reward.

Owing to this lack of understanding, progressive taxation has grown throughout the past century fed by such envy, which the great American poet Henry Wadsworth Longfellow called "the vice of republics."[4] Demagogues turn the law, which should protect the virtuous, into a tool for rewarding evil. To do so is to use the law to undermine its own purpose. Law is rightly an instrument of justice. Because the law is a teacher, using it to take from some simply because they have more than others inevitably sanctions this injustice. Such injustice has natural moral consequences.

This book explores the moral impact of tax policy. It is intended to help the reader better understand why tax policy decisions matter as social concerns. Though it is not an economic treatise, it does attempt to provide a coherent look at federal taxation.

The book opens by envisioning an approach to tax policy rooted in natural justice. It then traces the evolution of U.S. tax policy and assesses the American tax burden. Next it explores the fundamental problems with U.S. tax policy. As taxes and spending are inseparable, this book next provides a historical analysis of federal spending and of changing expectations of government. It offers a set of over-arching principles to guide the debate over fiscal reform. Finally, it guides the reader in applying those principles to tax policy proposals.

Section I

ONE

A Vision for Fiscal Reform

The swordsman plunged his weapon through the open window of the horse-drawn carriage. He slashed at the imprisoned priests, cutting the shoulder of one, slicing open the face of another, severing the hand of a third. His followers joined in, and the slaughter continued even as some of the frightened priests managed to escape. When the blood-drenched carriages finally reached their prison destination, a second mob killed most of the arriving survivors. Inside, prisoners trapped in their cells listened helplessly to the screams of the butchered and sent spies to the window to watch the massacre, knowing that their turn was coming soon. When those spies returned and reported that the victims who tried to shield themselves with their hands suffered the longest, as they often simply lost limbs first and then their heads, the waiting prisoners resolved to clasp their hands behind their backs when they too faced slaughter.

Born three years earlier of an attempt to alter the old political order and abolish the old social order, the French Revolution had degenerated into a bloodbath. The Revolution also became a soap opera of irony and absurdity that would be humorous if not for the horror of the bloody waters that carried it along from episode to episode.

In the space of ten years, France would see its king and queen beheaded and replaced by a dictator, who was himself later beheaded and replaced by an emperor. Citizens would be executed for a range of petty offenses, including sawing down a tree of liberty, furnishing sour wine to the defenders of the country, and weeping at the executions of others. Taxes would be abolished and reinstated, ministers dismissed and recalled. The Gregorian calendar and the common currency would be replaced.

The government of Paris established after the fall of the Bastille would be reorganized twice within fifteen months. The National Assembly would change its president every other week, and was often so entangled in such a web of resolutions and alternate resolutions, amendments and counter-amendments, that it couldn't figure out how to proceed. The inefficiency magnified the horror. No provision had been made for such an obvious need as removing the decapitated corpses piling up around the guillotine until a special commission was created to address the growing filth and stench.

The French Revolution had begun with a sweeping view of what it was against—the entire existing order. Its tragic flaw was that it had no clear vision of what it was for.

As French Revolution historian J.M. Thompson explains:

There was . . . no authorized programme, no accepted design for the new France. The revolutionaries had pulled down the old fabric before inquiring whether some parts of it might not be embodied in the new. The sovereignty had been transferred from the king to the people: but Louis XVI was still on the throne. The assembly was enacting, clause by clause, a new constitution: but each regulation had to make its way not merely against official obstruction, but against the age-long habits of a people unaccustomed to self-government. . . . But until the constitution was codified and enacted as a whole, it could not be said for certain—This is constitutional: that is not.[1]

Against this backdrop of directionless folly, the barbarity of human nature became the true sovereign. Because all the ecclesiastical, social, and political structures that restrained human barbarism were demolished without a coherent system to replace them, the French Revolution provides an unparalleled look at the toll of visionlessness.

To a far, far less extreme degree, United States fiscal policy has also fallen victim to visionlessness. Constitutionality has been rejected as a standard for weighing policy decisions; changes are implemented piecemeal in response to immediate demands. While the remnants of a Christian ethic, buttressed by restraining structures, have kept the United States from degenerating into the bloody horror of France during the Revolution, the United States has suffered from its failure to pursue public policy, including tax policy, according to a rational and coherent vision for a healthy American society. Indeed, there is a great deal of room between an optimal polity and the horror of the French Revolution, and the United States, while far from the latter, is also far from the former.

This chapter discusses the importance of vision in public policy, offers an example of a vision of a healthy American society, and explains why sound fiscal policy is necessary to achieving societal health.

A vision is a conception of what might be. It is vital to sound public policy because it illustrates the end purpose at which public policy is aimed. It burns away the fog that often hovers over public policy debate. By clarifying purpose, it provides a basis for discussion and a standard against which to weigh ideas and make decisions. When contrast with actual circumstances, it helps reveal problems and deficiencies.

By encouraging people to look beyond themselves and their immediate circumstances, vision helps ennoble and unify a people and a nation. It offers hope and inspiration, and in so doing it encourages sacrifice, protecting against the temptations of immediate desires. It solidifies purpose, and thereby calls up moral strength during long, hard seasons of despair. It protects individuals and nations from being satisfied with less than the best.

Sadly, United States fiscal policy offers an object lesson of what happens in the absence of vision. Today's fiscal policy is crafted with little regard to its ultimate effects. It is incoherent, fluctuating with competing interest group demands. It both exploits and exacerbates the human susceptibility to demagoguery. It has reduced a free people to moral slaves, squabbling over goodies.

Solving the problems fostered by fiscal policy forged without a guiding vision first requires establishing a coherent vision of the kind of society that public policy, including fiscal policy, should serve and support. To light the way to sound policy, the vision must be based on reality.

There is a natural order, and a realistic vision must be rooted in that order. In the natural order, virtue and vice each carries its own consequences. The consequences of virtue are largely positive. Hard work, patience, and humility tend to yield prosperity. Vice, on the other hand, brings negative consequences. Sloth, impatience, and self-centeredness tend toward suffering.

Because some individuals resist the natural order and seek to benefit themselves by injuring others, civil government has been instituted to maintain that order by protecting individual rights. To avoid undermining its own purpose, civil government should take pains not to disrupt the natural order. This principle applies especially to taxation, which has been instituted to provide government the economic resources required to perform its legitimate tasks. If through taxation it disrupts the natural order by creating all sorts of perverse incentives that infringe upon individual rights and overturn the natural consequences of virtue and vice, the government becomes part of the problem that it exists to quell — a contributor to social breakdown rather than an instrument of justice.

By providing a picture of what American life can be when government fulfills, rather than undermines, its proper purpose, sound vision can offer guidance for public policy decisions and help prevent policy makers from disrupting the natural order.

The following paragraphs offer a vision, rooted in natural order, of what America can be:

In a well-governed America, families are free to act according to their own values, in raising their children, in saving or spending money, in using time, in joy and sorrow, in hope and heartache, in need and in prosperity.

In this America, the sanctity of life and of the family is held in high honor. Marriage is esteemed as a sacred covenant, not denigrated as a means to financial goodies. Social power is seated within the home. The sense of obligation to family, church, and community is personal, not exercised through the mediating bureaucracy of the state.

Parents who so desire are free to care for their own children at home. Parents can teach the passive virtues, like obedience, contentment, and self-effacement, without fear of disadvantaging their children in a society dominated by special interest demands.

Children attend schools that teach the basics like reading and writing early enough to leave time for advanced science and mathematics, history, art and literature, and the quest for truth.

Families are free to make their own choices from among valid moral alternatives without the influences of public policy that steers behavior. Families can turn to pastors, family, and friends first for guidance when making major decisions, not to lawyers, accountants, and brokers. They run homes and businesses according to their own consciences. They can reach for and achieve their dreams without facing unnecessary barriers or vague apprehension about unknown barriers intentionally or unintentionally blocking success.

They enjoy the freedom to negotiate with employers or contract independently without government interference creating asymmetrical incentives. They are free to leave unsatisfying or abusive jobs without worrying about losing health coverage or other benefits. Their children can open lemonade stands without being shut down for failure to file forms. They enjoy the unadulterated freedom to dream that exists only in the absence of synthetic incentives.

Intact families living on honest wages in clean neighborhoods are the norm. They can afford decent living standards without assuming debt. They are confident in the rewards of hard work and responsible stewardship, and they can spend more time working for God and themselves than for the government.

These families are free to worship in whichever religious institutions they believe best teach and follow God's requirements for worship and righteous living and to look to these institutions, not the civil state, first for moral guidance, dispute resolution, and material support.

This great nation is loved, honored, and trusted enough for her citizens to respect the primacy of her founding documents. Law is made according to the standards set forth in the Constitution. It seeks long-term good over short-term gain. It upholds each individual as valued, capable, and morally free and responsible. The people are honest and optimistic enough to look critically at policies that fail and change them. Political power is properly understood and used as a tool to preserve and protect people and principle, not to perpetuate itself or aggrandize its stewards.

Government is servant, not master, fulfills its proper role, and is given due honor in it. It protects life and secures property while respecting the liberty of the people. Civil government wields the necessary power to punish law-breaking. Such power is concentrated at the local and state levels, not the federal level, because any government is most accountable when closest to its people. Law upholds what is right and enhances — rather than undermines — its own purpose, and sows respect for authority.

No goodies are distributed that discourage people from work and entrepreneurship, rewarding sloth, encouraging vice. Material needs are met by the free play of the market economy and, when necessary, by the voluntary contributions of individuals, families, and churches.

Wealth creation is understood as benefiting all in society, and those who improve lives by inventing new technologies and creating jobs are recognized as helping others, not resented as parasites living off those whose lifestyles they've enhanced. The natural rewards of virtue are left in place; the blessings of industry, planning, chastity, responsibility, delayed gratification, discipline, commitment, and stewardship are not mitigated by an intrusive state. These virtues are held in high esteem, not dismissed as frills that can be jettisoned on the journey toward a synthetic utopia. Vices like malice, envy, resentment, and ill will are seen as the social cancers they are, not the bases for policy goals.

Respect for others is the norm. The essential humanity, dignity, and rights of each individual are universally recognized. The people are secure enough in equality as a natural condition to encourage one another, not tear each other down. Babies in the womb, children playing in yards, students leaving libraries late at night, and grandparents on leisurely Sunday afternoon walks are safe.

In this America, daily life is not easy, but it offers more opportunity for fulfillment, hope, and joy than if it were, because these things are found in freedom and in virtue, in meeting challenges, overcoming obstacles, and reaching dreams.

In contrast to the difficult and joyous life of this vision, American life is increasingly oppressed by an overbearing civil government that fosters a sense of entitlement instead of responsibility, that sanctions selfishness and undermines respect, and that encourages immediate gratification over long-term good, as it sucks the blood from family, church, and community to feed its own insatiable lust for power.

The paradox of human nature enables this misuse of power and makes it difficult to reverse. Most people desire to be virtuous, yet often relent to the daily temptations of vice. They are morally frail creatures, and easily subject to temptation, to encouragement and discouragement. In the war between virtue and vice that rages in every human heart, vice has the natural advantage: it is easier; it feeds immediately felt desires, and the popular culture glorifies it. Adding economic incentive buttresses this natural advantage.

Perverse fiscal policy is only one cause of America's downward moral spiral, yet it is an important one. Years of expecting and depending upon government provision have left Americans docilely remitting $10,000 apiece to various levels of government. In the place of a healthy distrust of power is now a heavy dependence on an insatiable federal leviathan.

Fueled by higher and higher taxes, the U.S. government has shifted from establishing justice to overturning it, from ensuring domestic tranquility to presiding over an increasing incivility, from providing for the common defense to shrinking down that vital function in favor of mushrooming entitlement spending, from promoting the general welfare to kowtowing to special interest groups, and from securing the blessings of liberty to seizing the fruits of her people's labor.

The temptations of life in a state-sponsored bubble, free from the need to provide for one's self and one's family, from the risks of personal failure, from the knowledge that we're not entitled to anything, are real, but yielding to them means ultimately submitting to a lifetime of modern serfdom. America can do better. Reformed fiscal policy based on a sound vision that reflects the natural order is vital to restoring America's greatness.

Section II

TWO

Taxes and Revolution

An angry mob stormed down the dark streets of Boston toward the palatial home of Lieutenant Governor Thomas Hutchinson. Once there, they tore windows and doors from their frames and battered down walls. They got drunk in Hutchinson's wine cellar, destroyed the library, tossed a manuscript that Hutchinson had spent years drafting into the street, and chopped down the trees in his yard. They stole much of what they could, including the family silver and £900. When the break of dawn and the resulting fear of capture forced them to disperse, they were trying to tear off the roof. It was August 16, 1765. This mob violence was precipitated by the Stamp Act, through which the British Parliament had imposed new, internal taxes on the American colonies six months earlier.

Protests over the Stamp Act marked a milestone in colonial resistance to British control and in American tax history. Far beyond concern over mere shillings, the colonists were morally opposed to what they viewed as an inappropriate exercise of British power and the threat to colonial freedom. Thus the Stamp Act is a fitting opening point for this section, which traces U.S. tax history. It introduces the various federal taxes to which Americans have become subject, explores the ideas and events that led to their adoption, and demonstrates how they have increased over time.

Until 1765, all British taxes on the American colonies were external; in other words, they had applied to American commerce with the outside world. The Sugar Act of 1764 levied such a tax. At the time when the Sugar Act imposed modest taxes on a wide range of non-British goods, moral objection to British taxation was just beginning to percolate. With the threat to liberty posed by taxation looming, the colonists grew increasingly distrustful of Parliament. As Bernard Bailyn explains:

> The colonists universally agreed that man was by nature lustful, that he was utterly untrustworthy in power, unable to control his passion for domination. The antinomy of power and liberty was accepted as the central fact of politics, and with it the belief that power was aggressive, liberty passive, and that the duty of free men was to protect the latter and constrain the former.[1]

This distrust carried over to the colonists' perceptions of Parliament's justifications for new taxes. Viewing London lifestyles as profligate beside the harsh conditions of colonial life, the colonists suspected that tax revenues would be wasted. Though Britain had doubled its national debt in the French and Indian War, which was precipitated by the colonists, the Americans were unmoved by British claims that revenue increases were needed to pay off war debt. British claims that the revenues raised were for the protection of the colonists against Indian attacks met with equal suspicion; British regiments remaining in America were inexperienced in forest fighting and untrained for Indian attacks. Still, while resentment was beginning to brew, there was little practical resistance among the colonies outside New England, and most of it focused on the intrusive procedures intended to quell evasion rather than to the tax itself.

Resistance boiled over in 1765 when the British Parliament imposed the Stamp Act on the thirteen American colonies on March 22. Already popular in Europe, stamp taxes were levied on such items as newspapers, marriage licenses, almanacs, pamphlets, legal documents, business licenses, insurance policies, diplomas, dice, and playing cards. The taxes were paid by purchasing stamps to be affixed to the items taxed. Hoping to make the tax more palatable, Parliament granted colonists the exclusive right to sell the stamps; no British tax collectors would come to America.

It wasn't good enough. This was a tax on the internal activities of the colonists. To tolerate the Stamp Act would mean to tolerate the feel of British fingers on colonists' daily lives. Colonial legislatures held emergency sessions. The tax was condemned in town meetings, speeches, and pamphlets. Mob violence erupted in Massachusetts, New York, and Rhode Island. Tax collectors were burned and hanged in effigy. The homes and offices of British officials were destroyed. When the stamps arrived, no one would sell them. British governors wrote home that the rebellion could not be quelled. Leading the way to freedom, Massachusetts called for a congress of the colonies.

In early October, twenty-seven delegates from nine colonies held the Stamp Act Congress in New York. Its Declaration of Rights and Grievances asserted that taxes could justly be imposed only with the people's consent, declaring, "[I]t is inseparably essential to the freedom of a people, and the undoubted right of Englishmen, that no taxes be imposed on them but with their own consent, given personally, or by their representatives."[2]

Ironically, they were supported by a large number of British statesmen, including the Chancellor of the Exchequer, Lord Camden, who argued:

[T]axation and representation are inseparable — this position is founded on the laws of nature . . . it is itself an eternal law of nature, for whatever is a man's own, is absolutely his own; no man hath a right to take it from him without his consent, either expressed by himself or representative; whoever attempts to do it, attempts an injury; whoever does it, commits a robbery; he throws down and destroys the distinction between liberty and slavery.[3]

Thus, the modest amount of the tax (by today's standards) was not the issue inciting the colonists. Their fundamental objection was to the imposition of intrusive British power. This was about more than money; it was about freedom. As William Pitt warned, for the colonists to accept the Stamp Act would be to "voluntarily . . . submit to be slaves."[4]

One particular concern focused on the threat to religious freedom presented by the Stamp Act. The Act imposed taxes on ecclesiastical documents and, because only distributors selected by the British government were allowed to sell the officially stamped paper, some non-Anglican colonists feared that influential Anglicans could stop other churches from issuing such documents and even arrest their ministers if they violated the law.[5] Because the Act was introduced at a time when the British encouraged efforts by the Anglican hierarchy to establish the Church of England as a state religion within the colonies, much to the chagrin of members of other denominations, such threats were serious to the colonists. As the London-based *St. James Chronicle* allowed, "[S]tamping and episcopizing our colonies were understood to be only different branches of the same plan of power."[6]

Samuel Adams went further, viewing the Act as a threat to personal holiness: "I could not help fancying that the Stamp Act itself was contrived with a design only to inure the people to the habit of contemplating themselves as the slaves of men; and the transition from thence to a subjection to Satan, is mighty easy."[7]

The colonists were willing to make the sacrifices necessary to back up the sentiment. Two hundred New York merchants refused to order British goods until the Stamp Act was repealed. The traders of Philadelphia, Boston, Salem, and other port cities joined them.

The Act took effect on November 1, 1765. American business was disrupted, as little could be conducted without the stamps. Slowly it resumed without them. Meanwhile, thousands of workers in Manchester, Leeds, Nottingham, and other British industrial towns lost their jobs due to the American boycott of British merchandize.

Parliament finally repealed the law in February 1766, but the repeal was accompanied by passage of the Declaratory Act asserting its power to make laws over the American colonies, including those imposing taxes. At the time, most Americans were too preoccupied with rejoicing over the Stamp Act's repeal to take note of the Declaratory Act. Church bells rang; candles illuminated windows; guns blasted in celebration. The Sons of Liberty lit fireworks on Boston Common. Merchants immediately placed large orders for British goods.

The celebration did not long endure. By early 1767, the furor over the Stamp Act had quelled, and Parliament felt safe in imposing new taxes. It adopted the plan offered by Charles Townshend, chancellor of the exchequer, to levy import duties on a range of items used in the colonies, including paper, lead, glass, dyes, and tea.

To exacerbate the colonists' dismay, Parliament established a Board of Commissioners of Customs to enforce the Townshend duties and gave it Writs of Assistance. Writs of Assistance allowed tax officers to search for goods smuggled in order to evade import duties. An officer needed no judge or other official to endorse the writ; he could execute a search, with assistance from local police, on his own. Writs of Assistance were among the most hated features of British rule and a leading reason why the Founding Fathers enshrined protection from unreasonable search and seizure with the Fourth Amendment to the Constitution. James Otis, a brilliant young colonial lawyer, called them "the worst instrument of arbitrary power, the most destructive of English liberty and the fundamentals of law that ever was found in an English lawbook." He declared:

> [O]ne of the most essential branches of English liberty is the freedom of one's house. A man's house is his castle . . . whilst he is quiet, he is as well guarded as a prince in his castle. This writ, if it should be declared legal, would totally annihilate this privilege. Customhouse officers may enter our houses; we are commanded to permit their entry. Their menial servants may enter, may break locks, bars, and everything in their way . . . whether they break through malice or revenge, no man, no court, can inquire. Bare suspicion without oath is sufficient.[8]

Unwisely, Parliament appointed unpopular officials to the customs board and headquartered it in Boston, the center of opposition.

Full enforcement of the duties was impossible. By early 1769, merchants in every colony were refusing to import British goods. Many products, tea in particular, were smuggled in from other countries. Poorly paid customs officials survived on bribes. Those trying to execute their duties were frequently greeted at gunpoint. Friends and neighbors would surround the houses that officials tried to search for contraband. Colonists refused to testify against one another. In June 1768, a British customs official was locked in the cabin of John Hancock's sloop *Liberty* while the crew unloaded smuggled wine. When the customs board seized *Liberty*, violent uprising drove many of its members from Boston to the British garrison at Castle William. All told, there was only one smuggling conviction in New England in two and one-half years.

The Townshend duties also gave rise to a great deal of pamphleteering. Even Royalist moderate John Dickinson wrote in his *Letters from a Farmer in Pennsylvania*, "[W]e cannot be free without being secure in our property. . . . [W]e cannot be secure in our property if without our consent others may as by right take it away. . . . [T]axes imposed on us by Parliament do thus take it away."[9]

The British were in a quandary. The colonial boycott reduced exports to America by nearly £1,000,000 from 1768 to 1769, but to repeal the duties would be to back down again. Finally, in 1770, Parliament repealed most of the Townshend taxes, but retained the tax on tea. The smuggling of that product continued.

By 1773, 15–20 million pounds of unsold tea languished in British warehouses. British Prime Minister Lord North decided to reduce – but not repeal – the tea tax, thus underselling the smuggled Dutch tea, and export it to colonial merchants. The gesture was more than insufficient; it was offensive. The financial cost of the tax was not the issue inflaming the colonists. The true issue was the moral question of whether or not Britain had the right to tax the colonists at all without their consent. Attempting to undersell the smuggled tea was seen as an attempt at bribery. As one writer explained twenty years later, "[A] free people will not be amused by financial palliatives."[10]

Seven tea-carrying ships set sail: four for Boston and one each for New York, Philadelphia, and Charleston. Most of the New York merchants refused to stock the tea. The people of Philadelphia adopted resolutions declaring "the duty imposed by Parliament upon tea landed in America is a tax on the Americans, or levying contributions on them without their consent," and "it is the duty of every American to oppose this attempt."[11] The intimidated importers in those two cities sent the tea back. In Charleston, the tea was unloaded and then sat unsold in warehouses.

As usual, the patriots of Boston were rowdier. On the evening of December 16, a group of men disguised as Mohawks rowed out to the anchored tea ships, boarded them, split open the cargo chests, and dumped their contents – approximately £15,000 worth – into the harbor.

The British reacted to the Boston Tea Party in early 1774 with what became known as the Intolerable Acts. The port of Boston was ordered closed until the patriots made restitution for the tea. A new quartering act required families to lodge British soldiers in their homes. The Massachusetts Government Act made the colony's council and law-enforcement officers all appointive by the crown. The Administration of Justice Act permitted the transfer of any British official accused of committing an offense while on duty to be tried in England.

The Intolerable Acts were intended to make an example of Boston and intimidate the other colonies. They had the opposite effect: They unified the colonies. In Virginia, George Washington, who strongly opposed the

Boston Tea Party, argued that the colonies must not "suffer ourselves to be sacrificed by piece meals."[12]

The First Continental Congress opened in September 1774. In a long list of Parliamentary abuses of the colonies, the Congress first cited that the body had

> claimed a power of right to bind the people in the Colonies in North America by statutes in all cases whatsoever; and for carrying the said power into execution, has, by some statutes, expressly taxed the people of the said Colonies, and by divers other statutes under various pretences, but in fact for the purpose of raising a revenue, has imposed "rates and duties," payable in the said Colonies, established a Board of Commissioners, and extended the jurisdiction of Courts of Admiralty therein, for the collection of such "rates and duties."[13]

In other words, Parliament was unjustly exercising power over the colonies, including the power to tax.

The Congress asserted,

> [T]he power of making laws for ordering or regulating the internal polity of these Colonies, is, within the limits of each Colony, respectively and exclusively vested in the Provincial Legislature of such Colony. . . . [A]ll statutes for ordering or regulating the internal polity of the said Colonies, or any of them, in any manner in any case whatsoever, are illegal and void[14] and [A]ll statutes, for taxing the people of the said colonies, are illegal and void.[15]

On April 19, 1775, the Revolutionary War began at Lexington, Massachusetts. The American patriots under Gen. George Washington fought for more than six years through harsh weather, privation, and discouragement. Victory came on October 19, 1781, when General Cornwallis surrendered to General Washington at Yorktown. Soon afterward, peace negotiations began in Paris. A peace treaty was signed in November 1782 and ratified by Congress in April 1783.

THREE

A Newborn Nation

While the Revolutionary War raged on, Congress sought to create a government. Still struggling to throw off the yoke of tyranny, the founders of the United States of America were reluctant to empower a strong central government. Instead, they adopted the Articles of Confederation, which gave Congress power over foreign affairs, including war and peace, Indian issues, and not much else.

By the time the war ended, the new government faced a critical lack of revenue. The newborn nation had paid for her freedom fight by borrowing money. Most of the federal debt was owed to those who bought so-called continental bonds to be redeemed after the war. The government also owed France and Holland about $11 million. Unable to impose taxes to pay its war debt, the federal government could only ask each state to contribute. In 1782, Congress asked the states for $8 million; it received only $400,000. Not only could the government not pay its debts to other countries, it could not even pay its soldiers.

From their inception, Virginia's James Madison and New York's Alexander Hamilton considered the Articles inadequate. In a series of newspaper articles signed "The Continentalist," Hamilton called the new nation a collection of "petty states . . . jarring, jealous, and perverse."[1] Hamilton pointed to the lack of power to tax as the source of the fledgling government's impotence. "Power without revenue," he insisted, "is a name."[2]

Hamilton and other nationalists in Congress sought the power to levy a 5 percent import duty without having to go to the states for permission. As such power lay outside the limits of the Articles of Confederation, it could only be exercised with unanimous consent of all thirteen states.

Rhode Island held out on the grounds that state power to withhold taxes was "the most precious jewel of sovereignty." After Hamilton allowed in a January 1783 speech in Congress that he wanted national revenue collectors "pervading and uniting the States," Virginia withdrew her consent. Hamilton's plan was dead.[3]

One state that did take its war debt seriously was Massachusetts, which imposed heavy taxes on its citizens and incited a rebellion. As taxes rose, farm prices declined, making it harder for farmers to make ends meet. As a result, many Massachusetts farmers lost their land for non-payment of debt or taxes.

On August 1786, 1,500 angry men prevented the Hampshire County Court from meeting. A few weeks later, 200–400 men stopped a judge from entering a courthouse in Worcester. The insurgency spread quickly, and was attributed to the leadership of Daniel Shays, a former captain in the Continental Army. In January, Governor James Bowdoin sent 4,400 men to contain the rebellion. The rebels attacked the state troops at Springfield; Bowdoin's soldiers opened fire, killing four rebels; the rest fled.[4]

George Washington was appalled by Shays' Rebellion. "I am mortified beyond expression," he wrote a friend, "that in the moment of our acknowledged independence we should by our conduct verify the predictions of our transatlantic foe and render ourselves ridiculous and contemptible in the eyes of all Europe."[5] The nation's standing in the world was at stake.

In September 1786 Hamilton represented New York at a commercial conference of the States in Annapolis. Hamilton took advantage of the occasion to call for a constitutional convention that would "cement the Union." The Annapolis conference report looked forward to an "adjustment . . . of the Federal system" requiring the "united virtue and wisdom" of all the States.[6]

On May 25, 1787, a Constitutional Convention began the process of superseding the Articles of Confederation and adopting a Constitution. The fifty-five delegates were well read in history, law, and political philosophy, and they retained the recent memory of what they viewed as governmental tyranny. The document that emerged reflected these two different, but complementary, influences. Informed by both reason and experience, the new Constitution sought to empower the federal government to fulfill its responsibilities while still protecting the people from any future encroachments on their liberty. Thus its enumeration of powers fulfilled two functions: it explicitly granted specific authority to the government, and in so doing it also limited its power to what was granted.

The new Constitution set up a government of three branches: executive, legislative, and judicial.[7] Executive powers were to be embodied in a president, chosen by a college of electors. A judicial branch consisted of a Supreme Court and lower federal courts. The legislative branch comprised two houses: a House of Representatives, whose members were apportioned according to state populations and elected directly by the people whom they would represent; and a Senate, which comprised two members from each state elected by that state's legislature. Intended to be the body closest to the people, the House of Representatives alone was empowered to initiate tax legislation, in order to protect the people from excessive taxation.

Virginia's George Mason, the wealthy plantation owner who had drafted the Virginia Bill of Rights, on which the federal Bill of Rights would later be based argued that the small size of the Senate (twenty-six members) and the length of Senate terms (six years) made it "improper" for that body to enjoy the power of originating money bills. "An aristocratic body, like the screw in mechanics, working its way by slow degrees, and holding fast whatever it gains, should ever be suspected of an encroaching tendency. The purse strings should never be put into its hands," he declared.[8]

The Constitution created a federal government, meaning that it comprised a number of individual states endowed with inalienable powers of their own. By dividing powers among different branches and allowing each to undo the work of the others, the Framers of the Constitution built in a mechanism to prevent the government from becoming too powerful; this mechanism is called checks and balances. Realizing that the document was imperfect, they also included a procedure for amending it.

The Constitution declared itself, along with "the Laws of the United States which shall be made in Pursuance thereof" and all treaties made "under the Authority of the United States" to be "the supreme Law of the Land."[9] The Constitution was thus the document that both granted and limited the authority of the federal government. As only those federal laws that were in harmony with it were legitimate, it was the hinge on which liberty hung. Paradoxically, because the document that limits federal power also grants federal power, any attempt to ignore or overthrow its parameters in reckless pursuit of inconsistent legislation actually undermines the legitimacy of the government itself. If the Constitution's restrictions on federal power are invalid, so are its grants of authority.

Unlike the Articles of Confederation, the new document specifically granted the federal government the "Power to lay and collect Taxes, Duties, Imposts and Excises, to pay the Debts and provide for the common Defence and general Welfare of the United States" and mandated, "all Duties, Imposts and Excises shall be uniform throughout the United States."[4] (Duty ordinarily "means an indirect tax, imposed on the importation, exportation, or consumption of goods"; impost "signifies any tax, tribute, or duty, but it is seldom applied to any but the indirect taxes"; excises "are inland imposts, levied upon articles of manufacture and sale, and also upon licenses to pursue certain trades or to deal in certain commodities upon special privileges."[11] Samuel Johnson's eighteenth-century English dictionary is more colorful, if less baleful; it defines an excise as "a baleful tax levied upon commodities, and adjudged not by the common judges of property, but wretches hired by those to whom the excise is paid.")[12] The requirement that taxes be uniform, unanimously annexed on September 14, was intended to ensure equality and prevent discriminatory tax law.

One of the most bitter battles during the convention was over how state representation in the legislature would be apportioned: Would representation be proportional—meaning would large states have more representatives than small states—or would it be "equal"—with each state having the same number of representatives? The large states—Virginia, Pennsylvania, and Massachusetts—and the southern states—North Carolina, South Carolina, and Georgia, which expected soon to become large ones—sought proportional representation. The small states, fearing that their interests would otherwise be trampled, wanted equal representation. The bicameral structure of the legislature ultimately facilitated a compromise. After long and rancorous debate, it was agreed that the representation in the House of Representatives would be proportional. Later, the delegates agreed on equal representation in the Senate.

The Constitution also stipulates, "No capitation, or other direct, Tax shall be laid unless in Proportion to the Census or Enumeration herein before directed to be taken."[13] (A capitation tax, also known as a poll tax, is one of a fixed amount levied on every adult in a governed area. The Census was to be conducted every ten years in order to determine proportional representation in the House.) The words "or other direct" were inserted upon passage of a motion by Delaware nationalist George Read, who "was afraid that some liberty might otherwise be taken to saddle the States, with a readjustment by this rule, of past requisitions of Cong[ress] and that his amendment by giving another cast to the meaning would take away the pretext."

Though all but forgotten two hundred years later, the implied distinction between direct and indirect taxes was important. Though the distinction is informal rather than legal, tax historians and philosophers throughout the centuries have designated direct taxes as those that are levied directly against an individual, while indirect taxes are applied to commercial activity, such as sales. Income and property taxes, for example, are considered direct; customs duties and sales and selective excise taxes are considered indirect.

Though imprecise, the distinction was more than one of semantics. As early as ancient Greece, direct taxation was viewed as inimical to liberty, while indirect taxation was considered more compatible with its survival. Centuries later, Baron de Montesquieu, the French philosopher whose theory of the separation of powers was used by the Founding Fathers as the basis of our structure of government, explained: "A capitation is more natural to slavery; a duty on merchandise is more natural to liberty, by reason it has not so direct a relation to the person."[14]

The founders shared the view that direct taxes were dangerous and sought to protect the people by requiring that they be apportioned. The federal government would not be empowered to levy direct taxes on the people itself; rather each state would raise and remit to the national treasury an amount in proportion to its number of inhabitants.

The apportionment agreement served a more practical purpose as well. On July 12, 1787, Pennsylvania's eloquent Gouverneur Morris moved a proviso that direct taxation would be in proportion to representation. This would temper the large, wealthy states' quest for large representation—

and move the convention past a choke-point created by the competing demands of the large and small states.

Later, on July 24, Morris said that he had meant the clause proportioning direct taxation to representation "as a bridge to assist us over a certain gulph" and hoped the Committee would strike it out. On August 8, Morris, exasperated by southern demands that slaves be counted toward representation, argued against apportioning direct taxation to representation as "it is idle to suppose that the Gen[era]l Gove[rnmen]t can stretch its hand directly into the pockets of the people scattered over so vast a Country," and they could "only do it thru medium of exports[,] imports & excises." His point was that since the federal government would never be able to levy direct taxes immediately on the people themselves, the compromise was meaningless. It was too late. Though the compromise was altered in detail, its substance emerged in the Constitution.

Thanks to the general distrust of direct taxes, restricting them was relatively non-controversial. Such was not the case with the Constitution's prohibition on taxing exports. The fight over this issue was bitter and brutal, but the southern states, which relied heavily on export revenues and thus opposed export taxes, prevailed. The divisive moral issue of slavery still bore heavily on the debate.

Many northerners were outraged that the Constitution, drafted by the Committee of Detail charged with the project and delivered on August 6, 1787, expressly disallowed any prohibition on the importation of slaves but also prevented the taxing of exports. Slavery, Madison records Morris declaring,

> was a nefarious institution. It was the curse of heaven on the States where it prevailed. . . . What is the proposed compensation to the Northern States for a sacrifice of every principle of right, or every impulse of humanity[?] They are to bind themselves to march their militia for the defence of the S[outhern] States; for their defence ag[ain]st those very slaves of whom they complain. . . . The Legislature will have indefinite power to tax them by excises, and duties on imports: both of which will fall heavier on them than on the Southern inhabitants . . . the bohea tea used by a Northern freeman, will pay more tax than the whole consumption of the miserable slave,

which consists of nothing more than his physical subsistence and the rag that covers his nakedness. On the other side the Southern States are not to be restrained from importing fresh supplies of wretched Africans, at once to increase the danger of attack, and the difficulty of defence; nay they are to be encouraged to it by an assurance of having their votes in the Nat[iona]l Gov[ernmen]t increased in proportion, and are at the same to have their exports & their slaves exempt from all contributions for the public service.

In other words, the North was expected to tolerate the gross evil of slavery and the slave trade, while the South (by virtue of the three-fifths compromise, which counted three-fifths of slaves towards proportional representation in the House) would not only enjoy greater representation for basing its economy on the institution, but would not even have to pay taxes on the goods produced by slaves. Thus, the North would have to supply revenue needed to quell slave rebellions in the South.

On the other hand, the complex Massachusettsite Elbridge Gerry sided with the South in opposing export taxes. "Gerry thought the legislature could not be trusted with such a power," which "might be exercised partially, raising one and depressing another part of country," records Madison. Gerry warned that power over exports could be used "to compel the States to comply with the will of the Gen[era]l government, and to grant it any new powers which might be demanded. We have given it more power already than we know how will be exercised."

Morris, acknowledging that "[h]owever the legislative power may be formed, it will if disposed be able to ruin the country," countered that taxes on exports were a necessary source of revenue, as people would not have money to pay direct taxes for a long time.

John Francis Mercer of Maryland pointed out the behavior-altering property of taxation by arguing that export taxes were impolitic, encouraging the production of articles not meant for exportation. Connecticut's clumsy Calvinist Roger Sherman, acknowledging the same inevitability, argued that the complexity of business in America would render an equal tax on exports impractical and thought it wrong to tax exports except perhaps those articles that should not be exported.

On August 21, Connecticut's Oliver Ellsworth listed several moral reasons against Congress taxing exports:

1. [I]t will discourage industry, as taxes on imports discourage luxury.
2. The produce of different States is such as to prevent uniformity in such taxes. . . . There are indeed but a few articles that could be taxed at all . . . and a tax on these alone would be partial and unjust.
3. The taxing of exports would engender incurable jealousies.

Gouverneur Morris disagreed, and pointed out that taxing the exportation of raw materials would encourage domestic manufacturing.

Rather than a blanket prohibition on export taxes, Delaware's John Dickinson thought that it would be better to exempt particular articles from such taxes. Standing against the complexity that arises from efforts to juggle multiple interests in tax policy, Sherman argued it "best to prohibit the national legislature in all cases," as the "States will never give up all power over trade" and an "enumeration of particular articles would be difficult[,] invidious and improper."

Appealing to equality, George Mason pointed out that exports differed markedly throughout the states. Mason's South won when the clause "no tax shall be laid on exports" passed.

Immediately, the clearest effort to make use of the moral power of taxation came when Maryland's unkempt Luther Martin proposed to allow a prohibition or tax on the importation of slaves on the grounds that:

1. The three-fifths compromise encouraged slave trafficking;
2. "Slaves weakened one part of the union which other parts were bound to protect," rendering the privilege of importing them "unreasonable;"
3. "It was inconsistent with the principles of the revolution and dishonorable to American character to have such a feature in the Constitution."

Refusing to allow that the three-fifths compromise encouraged slave importation, rejecting the likelihood of slave insurrections, and releasing the other states from any obligation to protect the South from them, South Carolinian John Rutledge insisted that religion and humanity had nothing to do with the question and that interest alone was the governing principle with nations. Ellsworth asserted that morality or wisdom of slavery were considerations belonging to states.

Madison summarizes Mason's remarks the following day:

This infernal traffic originated in the avarice of British merchants. The British Gov[ernmen]t constantly checked the attempts of Virginia to put a stop to it. The present question concerns not the importing States alone but the whole Union. . . . He mentioned the dangerous insurrections of the slaves in Greece and Sicily; and the instructions given by Cromwell to the Commissioners sent to Virginia, to arm the servants & slaves, in case other means of obtaining its submission should fail. Maryland & Virginia . . . already prohibited the importation of slaves expressly. N[orth] Carolina had done the same in substance. All this would be in vain if S[outh] Carolina & Georgia be at liberty to import. The Western people are already calling out for slaves for their new lands, and will fill that Country with slaves if they can be got thro[ugh] S[outh] Carolina & Georgia. Slavery discourages arts & manufactures. The poor despise labor when performed by slaves. . . . They produce the most pernicious effect on manners. Every master of slaves is born a petty tyrant. They bring the judgment of heaven on a Country. As nations can not be rewarded or punished in the next world they must be in this. By an inevitable chain of causes & effects providence punishes national sins, by national calamities. . . . [T]he Gen[era]l Gov[ernmen]t should have power to prevent the increase of slavery.

Ellsworth responded that restricting slave importation would amount to unequal treatment among the states:

As slaves multiply so fast in Virginia & Maryland that it is cheaper to raise than import them, whilst in the sickly rice swamps foreign supplies are necessary . . . we shall be unjust towards S[outh] Carolina & Georgia. Let us not intermeddle. . . . Slavery in time will not be a speck in our Country. . . . As to the danger of insurrections . . . that will become a motive to the kind treatment of slaves.

As Madison records, South Carolina's Charles Pinckney took Ellsworth's argument a step further:

Virginia . . . will gain by stopping the importations. Her slaves will rise in value, & she has more than she wants. It would be unequal to require S[outh] C[arolina] & Georgia to confederate on such unequal terms. . . . He contended that the importation of slaves would be for the interest of the whole Union. The more slaves, the more produce to employ the carrying trade; The more consumption also, and the more of this, the more of revenue for the common treasury. He admitted it to be reasonable that slaves should be dutied like other imports.

Pennsylvania's James Wilson argued, "As the Section now stands, all articles imported are to be taxed. Slaves alone are exempt. This is in fact a bounty on that article."

Massachusetts' Rufus King "remarked on the exemption of slaves from duty whilst every other import was subjected to it, as an inequality that could not fail to strike the commercial sagacity of the North[er]n and middle States." Roger Sherman, on the other hand, opposed a tax on imported slaves as it made the matter worse by implying they were property.

Sherman's moral reasoning was not persuasive enough. Ultimately, the Constitution read: "The Migration or Importation of such Persons as any of the States now existing shall think proper to admit, shall not be prohibited by the Congress prior to the Year one thousand eight hundred and eight, but a Tax or duty may be imposed on such Importation, not exceeding ten dollars for each Person."[15]

From a moral perspective, this may have been the worst possible outcome. While the Constitution did allow the taxation of slaves, further diminishing them as human beings, the $10 per head limit was so small as to have minimal effect in actually reducing the slave trade. Such is often the case when moral issues are settled by compromise.

Once the new Constitution was drafted, it had to be ratified in state conventions. The quill pens that wrote it had scarcely been replaced in their wells when opponents, dubbed Anti-Federalists—although they considered themselves the true federalists, in contrast to the nationalists who sought a consolidated central government—began writing papers warning that the new Constitution gave the central government dangerous levels of power. Taxation was of particular concern.

In his third letter, the Federal Farmer, widely but controversially thought to be Virginia's Richard Henry Lee, warned against the large number of federal laws that would be required to enforce internal taxation and would overpower state governments:

A power to lay and collect taxes at discretion, is, in itself, of very great importance. By means of taxes, the government may command the whole or any part of the subject's property. Taxes may be of various kinds; but there is a strong distinction between external and internal taxes. External taxes are impost duties, which are laid on imported goods; they may usually be collected in a few seaport towns, and of a few individuals, though ultimately paid by the consumer; a few officers can collect them, and they can be carried no higher than trade will bear, or smuggling permit — that in the very nature of commerce, bounds are set to them. But internal taxes, as poll and land taxes, excises, duties on all written instruments, etc. may fix themselves on every person and species of property in the community; they may be carried to any lengths, and in proportion as they are extended, numerous officers must be employed to assess them, and to enforce the collection of them. . . . Internal taxation in this country is . . . important, as the country is so very extensive. As many assessors and collectors of federal taxes will be above three hundred miles from the seat of the federal government as will be less. Besides, to lay and collect internal taxes, in this extensive country, must require a great number of congressional ordinances, immediately operating upon the body of the people; these must continually interfere with the state laws, and thereby produce disorder and general dissatisfaction, till the one system of laws of the other, operating upon the same subjects, shall be abolished. These ordinances alone . . . will probably soon defeat the operations of the state laws and governments.

Should the general government think it politic, as some ad-ministrations (if not all) probably will, to look for a support in a system of influence, the government will take every occasion to multiply laws, and officers to execute them, considering these as so many necessary props for its own support. Should this system of policy be adopted, taxes more productive than impost duties will, probably, be wanted to support the government. . . . The internal sources of taxation then must be called into operation, and internal tax laws and federal assessors and collectors spread over this immense country. All these circumstances considered, is it wise, prudent, or safe, to vest the powers of laying and collecting internal taxes in the general government, while imperfectly organized and inadequate;

and to trust to amending it hereafter, and making it adequate to this purpose? It is not only unsafe but absurd to lodge power in a government before it is fitted to receive it[.]

When I recollect how lately congress, conventions, legislatures, and people contended in the cause of liberty, and carefully weighed the importance of taxation, I can scarcely believe we are serious in proposing to vest the powers of laying and collecting internal taxes in a government so imperfectly organized for such purposes. . . . I am sensible . . . that it is said that congress will not attempt to lay and collect internal taxes; that it is necessary for them to have the power, though it cannot probably be exercised. I admit that it is not probable that any prudent congress will attempt to lay and collect internal taxes, especially direct taxes: but this only proves, that the power would be improperly lodged in congress, and that it might be abused by imprudent and designing men.

Brutus, generally but questionably thought to be Robert Yates, wrote colorfully in his sixth letter that taxation would soon pervade every area of daily life:

The general legislature will be empowered to lay any tax they chuse [*sic*], to annex any penalties they please to the breach of their revenue laws; and to appoint as many officers as they may think proper to collect the taxes.

How far the power to lay and collect duties and excises may operate to dissolve the state governments, and oppress the people, it is impossible to say.

[T]he power to lay and collect duties and excises, would invest the Congress with authority to impose a duty and excise on every necessary and convenience of life.

This power, exercised without limitation, will introduce itself into every corner of the city, and country—It will wait upon the ladies at their toilett, and will not leave them in any of their domestic concerns; it will accompany them to the ball, the play, and the assembly; it will go with them when they visit, and will, on all occasions, sit beside them in their carriages, nor will it desert them even at church; it will enter the house of every gentleman, watch over his cellar, wait upon his cook in the kitchen, follow the servants into the parlour, preside over the table, and note down all he eats or drinks; it will attend him to his bed-chamber, and watch him while he sleeps; it will take cognizance of the professional man in his office, or his study; it will watch the merchant in the counting-house, or in his store; it will follow the mechanic to his shop, and in his work, and will haunt him in his family, and in his bed; it will be a constant companion of the industrious farmer in all his labour, it will be with him in the house, and in the field, observe the toil of his hands, and the sweat of his brow; it will penetrate into the most obscure cottage; and finally it will light upon the head of very person in the United States. To all these different classes of people, and in all these circumstances, in which it will attend them, the language in which it will address them, will be GIVE! GIVE! [emphasis in original]

In the same letter, Brutus warned against the unwarranted license Congress could assume via the general welfare clause:

It will be a matter of opinion, what tends to the general welfare; the Congress will be the only judges in the matter.

It is as absurd to say, that the power of Congress is limited by these general expressions, "to provide for the common safety, and general welfare," as it would be to say, that it would be limited, had the constitution said they should have power to lay taxes, &c. at will and pleasure. . . . [T]he government would always say, their measures were designed and calculated to promote the public good; there being no judge between them and the people, the rulers themselves must, and would always, judge for themselves.

[T]here are . . . favourers of this system, who admit that the power of the Congress under it, with respect to revenue, will exist without limitation, and contend that so it ought to be.

In his fifth letter, Brutus warned against the necessary and proper clause, especially in regard to taxation:

The design of the constitution is expressed in the preamble, to be, "in order to form a more perfect union, to establish justice, insure domestic tranquility, provide for the common defence, promote the general welfare, and secure the blessings of liberty to ourselves and posterity." These are the ends this government is to accomplish, and for which it is invested with certain powers, among these is the power "to make all laws which are necessary and proper for carrying into execution the foregoing powers, and all other powers vested by this constitution in the government of the United States, or in any department or officer thereof." . . . [T]he inference is naturally that the legislature will have an authority to make all laws which they shall judge necessary for the common safety, and to promote the general welfare. This amounts to a power to make laws at discretion.

[T]he power to lay and collect has great latitude; it will lead to the passing a vast number of laws, which may affect the personal rights of the citizens of the states, expose their property to fines and confiscation, and put their lives in jeopardy: it opens a door to the appointment of a swarm of revenue and excise officers to pr[e]y upon the honest and industrious part of the community, eat up their substance, and riot on the spoils of the country.

In the same letter, he warned against the insatiable appetite of direct taxes:

The distinction between external and internal taxes, is not a novel one in this country[;] it is a plain one, and easily understood. The first includes impost duties on all imported goods; this species of taxes it is proper should be laid by the general government; many reasons might be urged to shew that no danger is to be apprehended from their exercise of it. They may be collected in few places, and from few hands with certainty and expedition. But few officers are necessary to be [e]mployed in collecting them, and there is no danger of oppression in laying them, because, if they are laid higher than trade will bear, the merchants will cease importing, or smuggle their goods. . . . But the case is far otherwise with regard to direct taxes; these include poll taxes, land taxes, excises, duties on written instruments, on every thing we eat, drink, or wear; they take hold of very species of property, and come home to every man's house and packet. These are often so oppressive, as to grind the face of the poor, and render the lives of the common people a burden to them. . . . If the power of laying imposts will not be sufficient, some other specific mode of raising a revenue should have been assigned the general government; many may be suggested in which their power may be accurately defined and limited, and it would be much better to give them authority to lay and collect a duty on exports, not to exceed a certain rate per cent, than to have surrendered every kind of resource that the country has, to the complete abolition of the state governments, and which will introduce such an infinite number of laws and ordinances, fines and penalties, courts, and judges, collectors, and excisemen, that when a man can number them, he may enumerate the stars of Heaven.

In a competing series of letters known as the Federalist Papers, Alexander Hamilton, John Jay, and James Madison sought to defend the Constitution and to refute the anti-Federalists' charges.

In Federalist 36, Hamilton dismissed anti-federalist warnings against federal taxing power as alarmist and disingenuous: "Many spectres have been raised out of the power of internal taxation to excite apprehensions of people—double sets of revenue officers—duplication of their burthens by double taxes, and frightful forms of odious and oppressive poll taxes, have been played off with all the ingenious dexterity of political legerdemain." Holding the existence of both federal and state sets of tax laws and collectors unlikely, he insisted, "[T]he probability is, that the United States will either wholly abstain from the objects pre-occupied for local purposes, or will make use of the State officers and State regulations, for collecting the additional imposition."

In Federalist 31, Hamilton noted that the "antagonists of the proposed constitution . . . seem to make their principal and most zealous effort" against the "general power of taxation in national government." Implying that the lust for power could be contained by structure, Hamilton insisted, "[A]ll observations founded upon danger of usurpation, ought to be referred to composition and structure of government, not to the nature or extent of powers."

In Federalist 30, Hamilton claimed that American government had dwindled into a state of decay because it could not enforce the power to tax.

In Federalist 17, Hamilton insisted that the federal government would not compromise its own grandeur by meddling in state and local affairs:

Allowing the utmost latitude to the love of power . . . I confess I am at a loss to discover what temptation the persons entrusted with the administration of the general government could ever feel to divest the States of the authorities of that description. The regulation of the mere domestic police of a State appears to me to hold out slender allurements to ambition. . . . . The administration of private justice between the citizens of the same State, the supervision of agriculture and of other concerns of a similar nature, all those things in short which are proper to be provided for by a local legislation, can never be desirable cares of a general jurisdiction. It is therefore improbable that there should exist a disposition in the Foederal [*sic*] councils to usurp the powers with which they are connected. . . . . [T]he attempt to exercise those powers would be as troublesome as it would be nugatory . . . and the possession of them, for that reason, would contribute nothing to the dignity, to the importance, or to the splendour of the national government.

In the 35th letter, Hamilton argued that general latitude to tax anything at all would protect the people better than restricting the government to specified sources of revenue:

[I]f the jurisdiction of the national government in the article of revenue should be restricted to particular objects, it would naturally occasion an undue proportion of the public burthens to fall upon those objects. Two evils would spring from this source, the oppression of particular branches of industry, and an unequal distribution of the taxes, as well among the several States as among the citizens of the same State.

Elsewhere in the same letter, he implied that progressive taxation would never be imposed: "No tax can be laid on land which will not affect the proprietor of millions of acres as well as the proprietor of a single acre. Every land-holder will therefore have a common interest to keep the taxes on land as low as possible . . . common interest may always be reckoned upon as the surest bond of sympathy."

Later in the letter, expecting prudence to govern tax law, Hamilton wrote, "It might be demonstrated that the most productive system of finance will always be least burthensome."

Appealing to prudence in Federalist 12 as well, Hamilton wrote, "It is evident from the state of the country, from the habits of the people, from the experience we have had on the point itself, that it is impracticable to raise any very considerable sums by direct taxation."

Defending the much-feared necessary and proper clause in Federalist 33, Hamilton argued:

What is a power, but the ability or faculty of doing a thing? What is the ability to do a thing but the power of employing the *means* necessary to its execution? What is a LEGISLATIVE power but a power of making LAWS? What are the *means* to execute a LEGISLATIVE power but LAWS? What is the power of laying and collecting taxes but a *legislative power*, or a power of *making laws*, to lay and collect taxes? What are the proper means of executing such a power but *necessary* and *proper* laws?

This simple train of enquiry furnishes us at once with a test by which to judge of the true nature of the clause complained of. It conducts us to this palpable truth, that a power to lay and collect taxes must be a power to pass all laws *necessary* and *proper* for the execution of that power . . ." [emphasis in original]

In Federalist 44, Madison concurred. The necessary and proper clause, he wrote, "consists of the several powers and provisions by which efficacy is given to all rest. ... Without the *substance* of this power, the whole Constitution would be a dead letter." [emphasis in original]

In Federalist 62, Madison argued for the Constitution by making a compelling case for wise and stable government:

Every nation whose affairs betray a want of wisdom and stability, may calculate on every loss which can be sustained from the more systematic policy of its wiser neighbors.

The internal effects of a mutable policy are still more calamitous. It poisons the blessings of liberty itself. It will be of little avail to the people that the laws are made by men of their own choice, if the laws be so voluminous that they cannot be read, or so incoherent that they cannot be understood; if they be repealed or revised before they are promulgated, or undergo such incessant changes that no man who knows what the law is to-day can guess what it will be to-morrow. Law is defined to be a rule of action . . . how can that be a rule, which is little known and less fixed?

Another effect of instability is the unreasonable advantage it gives to the sagacious, the enterprising and the moneyed few, over the industrious and uninformed mass of the people. Every new regulation concerning commerce or revenue, or in any manner affecting the value of the different species of property, presents a new harvest to those who watch the change, and can trace its consequences; a harvest reared not by themselves but by the toils and cares of the great body of their fellow citizens. This is a state of things in which it may be said with some truth that laws are made for the *few* not for the *many*.

In another point of view great injury results from an unstable government. The want of confidence in the public councils damps every useful undertaking; the success and profit of which may depend on a continuance of existing arrangements. What prudent merchant will hazard his fortunes in any new branch of commerce, when he knows not but that his plans may be rendered unlawful before they can be executed? What farmer or manufacturer will lay himself out for the encouragement given to any particular cultivation or establishment, when he can have no assurance that his preparatory labors and advances will not render him a victim to inconstant government? In a word no great improvement or laudable enterprise, can go forward, which requires the auspices of a steady system of national policy.

[T]he most deplorable effect of all is that diminution of attachment and reverence which steals into the hearts of the people, towards a political system which betrays so many marks of infirmity, and disappoints so many of their flattering hopes. No government any more than an individual will long be respected, without being truly respectable, nor be truly respectable without possessing a certain portion of order and stability. [emphasis in original]

In the end, Madison and Hamilton won. With ratification by the ninth state, New Hampshire, on June 21, 1788, the new government was approved.

FOUR

Early Quarrels

The Congress of the United States of America under her new Constitution opened in New York City on March 4, 1789, but the body couldn't muster a quorom in both houses until a month later. The newborn nation remained deeply in debt and James Madison, now a member of the House of Representatives from Virginia, proposed a modest duty to supply more revenue. But despite the mounting need for revenue, passage was neither quick nor easy as different members sought to protect the economic interests of their constituents. In general, northern manufacturers wanted to protect the goods they refined while southern planters strove to protect the raw materials they exported from any retaliatory tariffs imposed by other countries.

Madison rose to debate on the House floor:

> I am afraid . . . on the one hand, that if we go fully in to a discussion of the subject, we shall consume more time than prudence would dictate to space; on the other hand, if we do not develope [*sic*] it, and see the principles on which we mutually act, we shall subject ourselves to great difficulties. . . . In the first place, I own myself the friend to a very free system of commerce, and hold it as a truth, that commercial shackles are generally unjust, oppressive, and impolitic; it is also a truth, that if industry and labor are left to take their own course, they will generally be directed to those objects which are the most productive, and this in a more certain and direct manner than the wisdom of the most enlightened legislature could point out. Nor do I think that the national interest is more promoted by such restrictions, than that the interest of individuals would be promoted

by legislative interference directing the particular application of its industry. For example, we should find no advantage in saying, that every man should be obliged to furnish himself, by his own labor, with those accommodations which depend on the mechanic arts, instead of employing his neighbor, who could do it for him on better terms. It would be of no advantage to the shoemaker to make his own clothes, to save the expense of the tailor's bill, nor of the tailor to make his own shoes, to save the expense of procuring them from the shoemaker. It would be better policy to suffer each of them to employ his talents in his own way. The case is the same between the exercise of the arts and agriculture — between the city and the country — and between city and town; each capable of making particular articles in abundance to supply the other: thus all are benefited by exchange, and the less this exchange is cramped by government, the greater are the proportions of benefit to each. The same argument holds between nation and nation, and between parts of the same nation.

If my general principle is a good one, that commerce ought to be free, and labor and industry left at large to find its proper object, the only thing which remains will be to discover the exceptions that do not come within the rule I have laid down.

The impost laid on trade for the purpose of obtaining revenue may . . . be considered as an exception: so far, therefore, as revenue can be more conveniently and certainly raised by this than any other method, without injury to the community, and its operation will be in due proportion to the consumption, which consumption is generally proportioned to the circumstances of individuals, I think sound policy dictates to use this mean[,] but it will be necessary to confine our attention at this time peculiarly to the object of revenue. . . .[1]

Madison was reminding his colleagues of how prosperity increases and of the importance not to impose laws, including taxes, which would depress wealth creation. However, he noted, there were some exceptions to this principle, one stemming from the fact that government had to raise revenue. Madison was in a difficult position. While he recognized the dangers of conflating revenue rising with economic isolationism, he wanted his bill to pass as soon as possible in order to flow some much-needed money into the Federal Treasury.

In the end, Congress reached a complicated compromise. A duty of 5 percent was applied to most goods, but certain products were taxed at much higher rates.[2]

Madison also targeted Great Britain, which had no commercial treaty with the United States but enjoyed more foreign trade with the new nation than any other. Madison proposed a mercantile system that would levy extra tonnage duties on foreign ships and an especially heavy duty on countries without such treaties. Secretary of the Treasury Hamilton, along with northern businessmen, opposed the plan. In the end, the only economic discrimination built into the Tonnage Act of 1789 was among American and foreign ships. American ships paid a duty of six cents per ton. American-built, foreign-owned ships paid thirty cents. Purely foreign ships paid fifty cents per ton.[3]

The disagreements heralded quarrels yet to come, quarrels arising from the differing interests of specific groups, the differing views of the proper function of taxes, and the differing philosophies about the appropriate scope of the federal government.

Though they had fought and written side by side in support of the Constitution, including the necessary and proper clause, the document had barely been ratified when Hamilton and Madison found themselves on opposite sides of what it meant. In 1790 Hamilton asked Congress for a bill to charter a national bank. "Every power vested in a Government," Hamilton wrote in a 15,000-word defense of his plan, "is in its nature sovereign and includes by force of the term a right to employ all the means requisite to the attainment of the ends of such power . . ."[4]

Madison was unequivocal in his opposition to Hamilton's idea. Hamilton's "latitude of interpretation," he insisted, was "condemned by the rule furnished by the Constitution itself," which listed the powers it conferred in order to limit them.[5]

The national bank was the centerpiece of Hamilton's fiscal plan to stabilize and stimulate the economy, which also called for the federal government to assume the states' debts. Hamilton favored "protecting duties" — which might be prohibitive in some cases — tariff exemptions for raw materials of manufacturing or rebates to manufacturers where duties had been levied for revenue or other purposes.[6] Some of Hamilton's tariff proposals were enacted in 1792.

Hamilton also proposed internal taxes, including an excise tax on "ardent spirits." Hamilton's goals went beyond simply seeking to raise revenue; he considered liquor a luxury, and one injurious to the moral well being of the nation, and sought to quell it.[7] In today's parlance, he advocated a sin tax.

A tax on distilled spirits passed in May 1971. Though considered an indirect tax, Hamilton's excise, like Parliament's Stamp Tax of three decades earlier, was an internal tax. While the Constitution explicitly granted Congress the power to impose such excises, provided that they be uniform, Hamilton's tax rankled nonetheless.

The tax was a heavy burden on farmers in the barter economy of the frontier, where cash was rare. These farmers used whiskey as money for trade. Grain was too bulky to transport across the mountains to the east, so they distilled it into whiskey, which they sold or bartered. Thus, the whiskey tax in practice became a 25 percent tax on money and trade,[8] a tax that had to be paid in cash, of which these farmers had little.[9]

Moreover, the forerunner of the Internal Revenue Service (IRS) was created to collect the tax. The country was divided into fourteen districts with as many directors. As with today's IRS, the incentives for collections were high. Each district director received 1 percent of the taxes collected in his district; each collection agent received 4 percent of the taxes he collected.[10] These tax collectors were granted power to enter cellars and barns to search for moonshine whiskey.[11] Naturally, citizens resented such intrusiveness.

Protest began peacefully when the tax was imposed in 1792, with the requisite meetings, speeches, and petitions. After two years, when a government born of tax revolts and established on the principle that a free people governs itself had not yielded to peaceful demands, simmering resentment exploded in violent revolt. Tax collectors and the sheriffs who sought to protect them were tarred and feathered. One revenue agent was met by a mob as he left his house; they held a knife to his throat and threatened to scalp and tar and feather him and burn down his house.[12] Someone calling himself "Tom the Tinker" shot the stills of farmers who paid the tax full of holes.[13]

Violence turned deadly when a tax official in Pittsburgh, learning what was happening to others, requested military protection. Eleven soldiers came from a nearby fort and were confronted by tax rebels. In the ensuing skirmish, three protesters were killed and four soldiers wounded. The soldiers surrendered, and the tax collector left town.[14]

A Supreme Court judge certified the existence of a state of insurrection in western Pennsylvania. Hamilton persuaded President Washington to call out the militia from four adjacent states. Washington himself led the 12,500 troops, in full dress uniform and with Hamilton at his side. This was the first and only time a sitting U.S. president has led troops in the field. The rebels surrendered, and an anti-tax committee signed an oath to submit to all U.S. laws in the future in exchange for pardons. A few of the rebels were tried in Philadelphia for treason. Two were convicted and sentenced to hang. Washington pardoned them and granted a general amnesty.[15] Having won the battle, the government quickly introduced more excise taxes on items including certain other liquors, carriages, snuff, sugar, salt, and auction proceeds.[16]

In fairness to Hamilton, debt must be paid, and, given the failure of external taxes to yield sufficient revenues, an excise tax was one of the least objectionable options. First, it was Constitutional, at least on the surface. Second, the tax was avoidable, again at least on the surface. As Hamilton explained, "The amount to be contributed by each citizen will in a degree be at his own option, and can be regulated by an attention to his resources . . ."[17] As the citizen was able to regulate his payment, Hamilton explained, "It is a signal advantage of taxes on articles of consumption that they contain in their own nature a security against excess."[18]

On the other hand, practical matters tempered the application of Hamilton's logic. As noted above, whiskey was not merely an article of consumption in western Pennsylvania, but it was also a medium of exchange, making it difficult for the people to minimize its use. Moreover, because the tax hit the farmers in this area harder than it did other citizens, they argued that it ran afoul of the Constitutional requirement that taxes be uniform, in other words, that it did not apply equally to all citizens. This concern illuminates the difficulty of applying Constitutional principle in tax practice. It is a difficulty with which the United States would wrestle again and again.

According to "country democrat" William Findley, the "people . . . firmly believed that the excise law was an immoral one. This theory became with many a religious principle."[19]

Moreover, the United States was born of the belief that taxation could not be imposed without the people's consent, either directly or through their representatives. For two years, the Whiskey Rebels peacefully made clear that they did not consent to Hamilton's excise. While the resulting violence may not have been justified, neither was the government's failure to respond to peaceful protest nor its use of military might to subdue a free people. The Whiskey Rebellion shows that the spirit of independence was alive in the early republic, but that it was now a threat to the new government it had birthed.

In the end, the rebels won, at least for a while. Having won the presidency by running on a platform including abolishing internal taxes, Thomas Jefferson in 1802 eliminated most of the excises.[20]

Prior to Jefferson's election, another major revenue crisis hit in the late 1790s. In the bitterly contested presidential election of 1796, Federalist John Adams, who made no secret of his antipathy toward France, narrowly defeated the anti-Federalist Francophile Jefferson. The French viewed Adams's election as an unfriendly act and responded by ordering that every impressed American found aboard a captured British ship be hanged. They expelled the United States Minister from France, cutting off diplomacy. The resulting undeclared naval war with France created unforeseen revenue needs for the United States, which sought to meet these needs by imposing its first estate tax. After the war ended, the tax was repealed in 1802.

Excise taxes returned in August 1813, when the United States was once again at war with Britain; they included duties on carriages, sugar refining, and distilled spirits, but they met with far less resistance this time. First, the taxes were specifically presented as war taxes to be repealed within one year following the end of the war. They were in fact repealed in 1817. Second, collection methods were far less imperial this time. Collectors were required to reside in the districts where they worked, and states were permitted to collect the amounts assigned to them and pay them directly into the Treasury in exchange for a 15 percent reduction of the amount due.[21]

After the War of 1812, the federal government returned to the tariff as its primary source of revenue.[22] The rise of new domestic industries during the war spawned clamor for increased isolationism. The Tariff of 1816, the first intended more for fencing domestic industries against foreign competition than for revenue, passed comfortably.[23]

Twelve years later, in 1828, the tariff would evolve once again into a political weapon, but, as is often the case with taxes used to injure a specific group, it would backfire on its originators. The saga begins with the bitter presidential election of 1824, which was thrown to the House of Representatives after none of the four candidates — Andrew Jackson, John Quincy Adams, Secretary of the Treasury William Crawford, and Speaker of the House Henry Clay — received a majority of votes in the Electoral College. Largely thanks to the support of Clay, who had garnered the fewest electoral votes and was thus no longer a viable candidate, John Quincy Adams won the contest with thirteen state votes. Almost immediately Jackson's supporters launched a campaign to elect their man next time around.[24]

The Jacksonians had no greater ally than the unwitting Adams himself, who outdid Hamilton in his grandiose notions for a strong central government and managed not only to rally his opponents but also to insult his constituents. Adams envisioned a central government that would promote internal improvements, establish a national university, finance scientific exploration, build astronomical observatories, improve agriculture, commerce, and manufactures, cultivate the arts and literature, reform the patent laws, and create a new Department of the Interior. To those who objected, Adams declared that his government would not "fold up our arms and proclaim to the world that we are palsied by the will of our constituents."[25]

The aging, but still acute, Thomas Jefferson was appalled and condemned the Federalists' "younger recruits, who, having nothing in them of the feelings or principles of '76, now look to a single and splendid government of an aristocracy, founded on banking institutions, and moneyed incorporation under the guise and cloak of . . . manufacturers, commerce, and navigation, riding and ruling over the plundered ploughman and beggared yeomanry."[26]

Taxation would play a key role in the political battle. The expansive Tariff of 1824 had levied higher duties on a broad range of items, providing a little protection for virtually every interest.[27] In 1827 a bill to hike the woolens duty failed with the tie-breaking vote of Vice President John C. Calhoun, a Jackson supporter who had previously supported the tariff.

Just as taxes can be used for the economic advantage of some over others, they can also be manipulated for political gain. Calhoun and his fellow Jacksonians proposed a tariff on raw materials so outrageously high that eastern manufacturers would be forced to vote it down. The scheme would allow Jackson men in the Northeast to claim credit for supporting the tariff while Jacksonians elsewhere could claim credit for opposing it, while Jackson himself remained above the fray.[29]

The scheme backfired against Calhoun when key Northeasterners supported it. New York's Martin Van Buren supported a compromise bone tossed to woolens manufacturers. Massachusetts Senator Daniel Webster flip-flopped his earlier opposition to protective tariffs, and defended his vote for the bill on the grounds that the woolens amendment made the bill more favorable to manufacturers. But he also cited "Other paramount decisions" — the upcoming election.

The bill, soon dubbed the Tariff of Abominations, passed in May 1828. Calhoun secretly drafted his Seminal Exposition the doctrine of nullification,[32] according to which any State could nullify an act of Congress it considered unconstitutional.

Despite the disastrous result of the political tariff game, in 1828 Andrew Jackson defeated incumbent president John Quincy Adams in a landslide. Calhoun remained as vice president and spent his short tenure fighting Secretary of State Van Buren to succeed Jackson.[33] But Calhoun's backfiring tariff game meant trouble in his backyard; South Carolina was in the throes of an agricultural depression, and most South Carolinians blamed the protective tariff. Calhoun proposed nullification to stop his state from seceding from the union. The nullification process, as Calhoun devised it, required a special state convention to declare a law unconstitutional, a breach of the original compact among the states, and thus null and void. South Carolinians argued that the Constitution authorized tariffs for revenue only, not for economic protectionism, but the state held off on nullification or other action against the tariff in the hopes of a more palatable policy from the Jackson administration.

At Jackson's request, the Tariffs of 1830 and 1832 did cut rates, but South Carolina was not satisfied. In November 1832, a state convention adopted an ordinance of nullification, which declared the Tariffs of 1828 and 1832 to be unconstitutional and prohibited their collection within the state after February 1, 1833. The state legislature also elected Calhoun as Senator and he resigned as Vice President in order to defend his nullification doctrine on the Senate floor.[34]

Henry Clay proposed a compromise that would reduce the tariff. Congress passed Clay's compromise and a Force Bill, which authorized Jackson to use the army to force South Carolina to obey federal law. South Carolina rescinded its nullification of the tariff and nullified the Force Law.[35]

From the first measure introduced in the first Congress, quarrels, both verbal and violent, over tariffs and excises illustrate the complex jumble of practical and principled concerns that arise from taxation and the temptations for special-interest gain that it encourages. These concerns grow only more complicated as government imposes a greater array of taxes.

FIVE

The Income Tax versus the Constitution

Primary reliance on tariffs for revenue changed with the Civil War. As the war raged on, collections of customs duties were at a near halt, largely due to the blockade efforts of the Confederate Navy. The government resorted to borrowing. In August 1861, the Union government imposed the first federal income tax in American history, which levied a rate of 3 percent on annual incomes over $800.[1]

The next year, Congress passed the Internal Revenue Act of 1862. This legislation was the most comprehensive, far-reaching tax measure up to that point in U.S. history. Every manufactured article was subjected to excise taxes, as were the gross receipts of railroads, ferryboats, steamships, toll bridges, and advertisers. It imposed an inheritance tax, license fees, and stamp duties.[2] Finally, it raised and graduate the income tax, imposing a rate of 3 percent on annual incomes from $600 to $10,000 and a marginal rate of 5 percent on amounts above $10,000.[3]

The inheritance tax required those who received legacies and personal property from estates worth more than $1,000 to pay a graduated tax based on relationship to the deceased. Rates ranged from .75 percent for ancestors, lineal descendants, and siblings to 5 percent for distant kin and non-relatives. (An inheritance tax is distinct from an estate tax, which, if graduated, is so on the basis of value of the estate, rather than relationship to the deceased.)[4]

Once having introduced taxes on such an expansive array of activities, from working to spending to dying, Congress was able to raise them. The Internal Revenue Act of 1864, raised tax rates on distilled spirits from 20 cents to $1.50 per gallon, ten times the original cost of the product. The tax on loose tobacco more than doubled, and the tax on cigars increased from

$3.50 to $40.00 per thousand.[5] Inheritance taxes were also increased, and a succession tax was applied to persons inheriting real estate. The income tax went up again, to 5 percent on incomes between $600 and $5,000, 7.5 percent on incomes of $5,000 to $10,000, and 10 percent on higher incomes.[6]

Conforming to precedent, most of the new taxes were abolished after the War ended. The inheritance tax was repealed in 1870. The income tax was repealed in 1872. Most of the excise taxes were repealed in 1867 and 1870, but the liquor and tobacco taxes remain to this day[7] (except for liquor during the Prohibition Era).

In the meantime, though, a taxpayer had challenged the Constitutionality of the death tax by contending that it was a direct tax and thus must be apportioned. Though the court didn't settle the case of *Scholey v. Rew* until 1874, four years after the tax was repealed, it decided against the taxpayer, ruling that death taxes were indirect and did not have to be apportioned.[8]

In addition to the remaining excise taxes, the government from that point fueled itself with tariffs on foreign goods and the sale of public lands. Through this point, taxes were levied in order to fund the various government functions allowed under the Constitution, such as fighting wars, repaying debt, and delivering mail. Drafted by men well-educated in law, history, and philosophy, designed to both empower and restrain federal government, and founded on the western principles of government developed over centuries, the Constitution was recognized for roughly a century as the final word on what the government should do and for what purposes and by what means taxes could be raised.

Respect for Constitutional limits began to diminish with the Civil War. While the income tax was repealed after the war's end, the precedent of taxing incomes had been established. Agitation for reinstating the income tax began almost immediately after its repeal, but proposals were easily defeated. The 1880s were a prosperous time, and already existing taxes yielded annual surpluses of more than $100 million.[9]

At the same time, though, southern and western farmers began to resent more and more the increasing wealth of eastern businessmen. The balance of economic power was shifting from farms to factories, and farmers sought to use the power of government to strengthen their relative economic position. The platform of the 1892 Populist convention in Omaha,

Nebraska, decried the "vast conspiracy against mankind" threatening the nation with "moral, political, and material ruin." Specifically, the complaint was unequal wealth distribution: Land and wealth were concentrated "in the hands of capitalists" accumulating "colossal fortunes." Though the Populists never won a presidential election, they were popular enough to win congressional seats and gubernatorial mansions, and they exerted influence from these posts. And their ideas, weaving their way into people's minds, had consequences.

Until this point, with a few exceptions, taxes were imposed primarily to raise revenue. That changed in the late 1800s when income taxes were supported and imposed primarily to spread the wealth around. As economic historian Robert Higgs explains, "The income tax was seen by proponents and opponents alike as an instrument of redistribution; in the parlance of time, it was 'class legislation.'"[10]

The idea of taxing the rich is a politically powerful one, as it can easily be couched in emotional, ersatz moral, rhetoric, and this minority does not have the voting power to stop it from being imposed by the non-rich majority. Public acceptance of the power of the majority to impose taxes upon the minority has held firm for a century and is the basis of every effort to oppose marginal rate reductions as "tax cuts for the rich." This tyranny of the majority violates the principle of taxation only with consent upon which the United States was founded. It is exactly the kind of rule by faction that James Madison warned about, where "measures are . . . decided, not according to the rules of justice and the rights of the minor party, but by the superior force of an interested and overbearing majority."[11]

As the Industrial Revolution gained steam, populism gave way to progressivism, which can be viewed as the umbrella for many groups whose common tie was a commitment to using the state as an activist for social change, rather than as an impartial enforcer of justice.[12]

First was the business reform movement. Centuries of agrarian society in both the Old and the New Worlds had ingrained the idea that work yields ownership, personal freedom, and control. As more and more people began to work at industrial jobs, work no longer yielded these things, but simply wages. Industrial owners came to be seen as taking the fruits of others' labor while violating their personal liberty.

At this time, significant numbers of people began turning to the federal government to protect them from this perceived violation. The United States was a nation born of people seeking escape from oppression and founded on the premise that government exists to secure the rights of the people. Now the perceived enemy was not an oppressive foreign country but the industrial giants of our own, yet the cry for protection by the government arose nonetheless.

While some progressives were unabashed socialists, most stopped short of calling for outright government ownership and control of businesses, preferring instead that companies be privately owned and operated, but regulated by the federal government, diminishing private power while expanding that of the government.

Rejecting the view of government as a potential tyrant, "as Jefferson did," wrote Theodore Roosevelt's friend Henry L. Stimson, "we now look to executive action to protect the individual citizen against the oppression of this unofficial power of business."[13] As historian Arthur M. Schlesinger, Jr., put it, "For national government to do its job, it had to be stronger than any private group in society."[14] This movement's successes included child labor laws, the minimum wage, and the eight-hour workday.

A second movement within progressivism was the government reform movement. Broadly, this branch sought to make government more accountable and more efficient. The effort to make government more accountable achieved some notable successes—ranging from municipal reform to women's suffrage. Its efforts to make government more efficient—imposing professional administrators such as city managers and centralizing decision-making authority within government—were also successful. Regrettably for the reformers, these successes were somewhat at odds with each other, as transferring power from elected officials to unelected bureaucrats and centralizing authority actually made government less accountable.

A third movement was the social welfare movement, which sought to aid the urban poor through poverty alleviation efforts. While these efforts were locally based in the beginning, they would soon grow into massive federal programs.

A fourth movement was the social control movement, which sought moral reform, now more popular than ever as more people, especially the young, were flocking to cities. The most notable achievement of this wing was Prohibition.

What all these movements had in common was the belief that government could and should fill an active, involved role in solving people's problems. Because such a role required an expanding government, Progressives sought to discredit the Constitution, which limited government. Motivated by economic interests, they attacked the Constitution as a tool of economic injustice.

Progressive J. Allen Smith claimed, "[T]he Constitution was in form a political document, but its significance was mainly economic. It was the outcome of an organized movement on the part of a class to surround themselves with legal and constitutional guarantees which would check the tendency toward democratic legislation."[15] In other words, the Constitution was motivated by economic selfishness and designed to protect only the rich and powerful. The Progressives, in contrast, sought to empower the majority through economic redistribution. The centerpiece of this agenda was the progressive income tax.

Because their agenda included expanding government, the Progressives specifically targeted the doctrine of checks and balances, the Constitutional mechanism under which each branch of government was prevented by the other two from amassing inappropriate power, and with it the idea of government restrained by a Constitution. Woodrow Wilson wrote:

> Government is not a machine, but a living thing. It falls, not under the theory of the universe, but under the theory of organic life. It is accountable to Darwin, not to Newton. It is modified by its environment, necessitated by its tasks, shaped to its functions by the sheer pressure of life. No living thing can have its organs offset against each other as checks, and live. On the contrary, its life is dependent upon their quick cooperation, their ready response to the commands of instinct or intelligence, the amicable community of purpose. Living political constitutions must be Darwinian in structure and in practice.[16]

Perhaps the greatest irony of the Progressive legacy is that the movement's judgments against the Constitution and the motives that underlay it would never have enjoyed the slightest credence in any but the republican form of government that it established. Only in a nation dedicated to the principles of equality of and liberty for all could complaints resonate that some were economically advantaged over others. The Progressives' arguments against the motives for the Constitution, colored by their own economic lenses, could not have been successful without the prior acceptance of the ideals of the American founding. Regrettably, the irony was lost on many at the time and throughout the century that followed, and Progressive ideas fundamentally reshaped American public policy.

Though they caused themselves and the rest of the nation great economic pain in the process and its aftermath, the Progressives eventually won out. Agitating for inflationary monetary policies such as the repeal of the gold standard, in order to enable themselves to pay their debts with inflated dollars and obligate the federal government to buy silver, western and southern farmers ignited a run on gold and contributed to the Panic of 1893. The ensuing depression, which continued for four years, caused a drop in tax revenue and created favorable political conditions for the reimposition of the income tax.

In 1894 a progressive income tax bill was sharply debated in both houses of Congress. Opening the debate in the Senate was a prophetic David Hill (D-N.Y.), who argued that the tax was unnecessary, constituted class legislation in that its entire burden would afflict a minute number of citizens, would cause economic ruin by dampening incentive and lowering wages, would be inquisitorial and invite fraud and corruption, would be unequally borne by the states, and represented an ill-advised effort to follow Europe down the path to socialism.[17]

Reasoned and prophetic argument was inadequate to quench the flames of resentment. The fledgling envy lobby scored its first major victory in 1894 when Congress imposed America's first peacetime income tax of 2 percent on incomes above $4,000, exempting 98 percent of the people. The act included gifts and inheritances as income. Former federal judge John F. Dillon denounced the scheme as "a forced contribution from the rich for the benefit of the poor," "class legislation of the most pronounced and vicious type," "violative of the constitutional rights of the property owner, subversive of the existing social polity, and essentially revolutionary."[18]

The envy lobby didn't rejoice for long. Almost immediately the income tax was brought before the Supreme Court. One lawyer pointed out that the tax rate might rise from 2 percent to as high as 20 percent. Another argued: "[T]he fundamental principle at stake was whether or not the United States would be a land of equality in taxation, for once it is decided that the many can tax the few, it will be impossible to take a backward step."[19]

Attorney Joseph H. Choate argued before the Court, "The act of Congress which we are impugning before you is communistic in its purposes and tendencies, and is defended here upon principles as communistic, socialistic—what shall I call them—populistic as ever have been addressed to any political assembly in the world."[20]

The lasting impact of the case was summed up in Choate's closing argument: "No member of this court will live long enough to hear a case which will involve a question more important than this, the preservation of the fundamental rights of private property and equality before the law, and the ability of the people of the United States to rely upon the guarantees of the Constitution. . . . There is protection now or never." Choate concluded, "You cannot hereafter exercise any check if you now say that Congress is untrammelled and uncontrollable."[21]

The issue at stake was more than simply economic. At its heart, the Court was being asked to decide whether the majority could impose a specific law against a minority. The year after it was imposed, the Supreme Court declared the tax unconstitutional by a five-four vote. The Court held that the income tax was a direct tax and must be apportioned among the states by population.

The Court was divided on the question of uniformity; Justice Stephen Field wrote a concurring opinion declaring that the tax was non-uniform in that it exempted 98 percent of the population. He wrote, "Such favoritism could make no pretense to equality; it would lack the semblance of legitimate tax legislation,"[22] and warned, "'If the Court sanctions the power of discriminating taxation, and nullifies the uniformity mandate of the Constitution . . . it will mark the hour when the sure decadence of our present government will commence.'"[23] Field's prophetic opinion anticipated the class warfare of the twentieth century: "Congress, where is the course of usurpation to end? The present assault upon capital is but the beginning. It will be but the stepping-stone to others, larger and more sweeping, till our political contests will become a war of the poor against the rich; a war constantly growing in intensity and bitterness."[24]

Citizens remained secure from progressive taxation until 1898, when the Spanish-American War led to another death tax. Ranging from .74 percent to 15 percent, the tax was imposed on the value of personal property in gross estates, with estates under $10,000 and property passing to widow(er)s excluded.

The following year, the Supreme Court dismissed warnings of future danger to democracy presented by the estate tax's progressive rates and approved the scheme in *Knowlton v. Moore*: "The grave consequences which it is asserted must arise in the future if the right to levy a progressive tax be recognized involves in its ultimate aspect the mere assertion that free and representative government is a failure, and that the grossest abuses of power are foreshadowed."[25] Despite the Supreme Court, the estate tax was repealed in 1902.

The envy lobby didn't give up. Robert Higgs explains, "Many people of smal means and limited accomplishments resent the rich and successful capitalists (whose conspicuous consumption helped . . . fuel these fires); less successful men relish the idea of cutting tycoons down to size."[26]

In 1909, the 16th Amendment to the Constitution, authorizing a federal income tax, was proposed. That same year, Virginia enacted an income tax, but huge numbers of people refused to pay it. Tax agents went into rural counties to collect it and were never heard from again. The tax was repealed the following year after less than $100,000 was collected.[27]

The federal government, which had better enforcement machinery, was undaunted by Virginia's experience. Buoyed by assurances that income tax rates would never exceed a few percentage points, the federal amendment passed in 1913.[28] That same year, progressive rhetorical assault on the Constitution reached a new low with the publication of *An Economic Interpretation of the Constitution of the United States* by Professor Charles Beard of Columbia University, who sought "to expose the undemocratic nature of the Constitution, to unmask its hidden features in order to show that it deserved no veneration, no respect, and should carry no authority to democratic Americans of the twentieth century."[29]

The new income tax was first imposed on October 3, 1913. It dictated a base rate of 1 percent on income up to $20,000; from there, marginal rates went up to 7 percent on income over $500,000. In other words, a citizen paid 1 percent on the first $20,000 of his taxable income. From there, his tax rate rose along with his income to a top rate of 7 percent assessed on any income over and above $500,000. In addition, the first $3,000 for single filers or $4,000 for married couples was exempt from taxation. In other words, a married couple did not have to pay any income tax until they earned $4,000. Families also enjoyed a $500 per child deduction.

About 350,000 people were subject to the tax. The new form 1040 was four pages long. A number of sources of income were excluded: interest on state and local bonds, salaries of state and local employees, the income of the president and federal judges, gifts and inheritances, and life insurance proceeds.[30] In addition, there were six categories of deductions: business expenses, interest on personal debt, other taxes, casualty losses, bad debts, and depreciation of business property. Since they weren't paying it, most Americans were fairly content with the tax.

The tax code quickly became more complex. By 1915, some congressmen were unable to complete the forms because they were too confusing. One member explained why the code became so unfathomable: "I write a law. You drill a hole in it. I plug the hole. You drill a hole in my plug."[31] In other words, Congress passes a tax law; somebody finds a loophole; Congress passes another law to close the loophole; somebody finds a loophole in the new law, *ad infinitum* (and *ad nauseum*).

SIX

The Century of Taxes

The 16th Amendment spawned enormous government growth. Amending the Constitution to allow the progressive income tax meant chiseling cracks into the principles of justice that originally prohibited the scheme. In those cracks, the rationalization of resentment-based fiscal policy grew like mildew. And once given a home, that smug rationalization, like mildew, swiftly spread, frustrating the efforts of the morally fastidious trying to bleach it away.

Shortly after the tax was first imposed, the increasing revenue demands created by World War I helped obscure the questionable intentions of those who supported it as a means of enforcing synthetic economic egalitarianism. The Great War was a watershed moment for the income tax in America. Because the war reduced imports, it also reduced the revenues from customs duties. This created enormous revenue demands, especially once the United States had become a belligerent. The easiest solution was to raise the income tax. While there was some reduction in the tax after the war, it has never returned to its pre-war levels. Once politicians saw its tremendous revenue-yielding capacity, the income tax was irrevocably enshrined in America's political landscape.

Within four years, a relatively modest tax with a large $4,000 exemption for families and a maximum rate of 7 percent, which had produced a negligible share of tax revenue, saw its exemption plunge to $1,000, and its highest rate soar ten-fold to 77 percent. This meant that families would have to pay taxes after the first $1,000 of income and that some people were subject to a marginal tax rate of 77 percent. Even the lawyer who warned the Supreme Court of an impending 20 percent bracket just two decades earlier hadn't foreseen such skyrocketing rates.

The Revenue Act of 1916 included an estate tax with many of the same features of today's system. Graduated tax rates were applied to the net estate (i.e., gross estate minus deductions). After an exemption of $50,000, tax rates started at 1 percent and rose to 10 percent on estates worth more than $5 million.[1] In 1917 estate tax rates were more than doubled and two more brackets were added. In 1918, Congress reduced the rates on estates under $1 million and allowed deductions for charitable contributions, but it expanded the tax base, loosening its grasp with one hand but gripping tighter with the other.

Americans enjoyed mild temporary relief as income taxes were reduced after the war. The Revenue Acts of 1921, 1924, and 1926 reduced the top income tax rate to 25 percent. In response, the economy expanded, growing 59 percent between 1921 and 1929. Personal income tax revenues increased substantially during the same time period, rising from $719 million in 1921 to $1,160 million in 1928, an increase of more than 61 percent. Taxes paid by those making $50,000 or more rose from 44.2 percent of the total tax burden in 1921 to 78.4 percent in 1928.[2] The prosperity nurtured by tax cuts accomplished what exorbitant rates could not: raising revenue.

But that prosperity drew envious eyes once again toward large fortunes in those *Great Gatsby* days. In 1924 Congress increased the top marginal rate on estates worth $10 million or more to 40 percent and added a gift tax with the same rate schedule along with exclusions of $50,000 over a lifetime and $500 for each donee each year. This meant that an individual could give up to $50,000 over his lifetime or $500 annually to each of an unlimited number of others without these gifts being subject to the gift tax. The gift tax was introduced to prevent people from avoiding estate taxes by transferring assets before death; it is assessed at the time of transfer made by a living person. The gift tax is cumulative, meaning that each gift is added to earlier gifts for tax purposes.

Just two years later in 1926, backlash against such government greed was so severe that Congress had to cut the top rate down to 20 percent and increase the exemption to $100,000. Congress also repealed the gift tax. In 1929, the Supreme Court ruled in *Bromley v. McCaughn* that the gift tax was an excise tax, meaning that it was considered indirect and therefore Constitutional.[3]

Then the Great Depression hit, thanks in part to the Fordney-McCumber Tariff of 1922 and the Smoot-Hawley Tariff of 1930. Income taxes spiked sharply from 24 percent in 1929 to 63 percent by 1932, lengthening and deepening the Depression. Under the Revenue Act of 1932, income tax rates were raised virtually across the board, but especially on lower- and middle-income earners. Personal income tax exemptions were dramatically reduced, while the base and marginal rates were sharply raised.[4]

In 1932 Congress also imposed a three-fold estate tax increase, which raised its rates, cut the exemption level in half to $50,000, and added two new brackets. The gift tax was also reintroduced with rates set at 75 percent of those of the estate tax. An expanded list of excise taxes was also imposed and the existing ones raised; while some were shortly repealed, most remained throughout the decade.[5] Congress pushed further down this slippery slope during the Great Depression by raising the rates and expanding the estate-tax base. In 1934 the top estate tax rate was increased to 60 percent on estates worth more than $10 million. By 1935, the top estate tax rate was 70 percent on estates worth more than $50 million.

President Franklin Delano Roosevelt justified the redistributive intent of the Revenue Act of 1935, which increased the top income tax rate from 63 percent to 79 percent, on the grounds that it would short-circuit the even more activist redistribution policies being propounded by Huey Long and others. To combat these "crackpot ideas," Roosevelt rationalized, "it may be necessary to throw to the wolves the forty-six men who are reported to have incomes in excess of one million dollars per year."[6] Tax revenues plummeted in response[7] to Roosevelt's salvage-fiscal-sanity by jettisoning-fiscal-sanity strategy.

In addition, workers in the 1930s became subject to a new kind of tax: the payroll tax. Although it is also imposed on wages, the payroll tax is different from the income tax. Half the payroll tax is paid by the employee, and half is paid by his employer (at least in theory). The employee's share is taken directly out of his paycheck. There are no exemptions, deductions, or credits. It is assessed on the first dollar of wages up to an annually changing limit at a flat rate, which is also subject to change. Payroll taxes are not deductible on federal income tax returns. That means that workers are taxed twice on the same earnings or, in other words, taxed on money that they never received because it was already taxed away, rather like making payments on a new car totaled by a drunk driver on the way home from the dealership.

There are several types of payroll taxes. Largest are those earmarked for Social Security and Medicare. In 1995 the $447 billion collected for these two programs accounted for one-third of federal revenue. Other payroll taxes that finance programs like unemployment benefits and railroad retirement accounted for 2.8 percent of federal revenues.[8] When the Social Security system took effect in 1937, the actual payroll tax rate, including both employee and employer shares, was 2 percent.[9] It applied only to the first $3,000 of wages.[10] Both the rate and the cap would climb.

On top of the Depression came World War II, which took the income tax from a tax on the wealthy to one on the middle class. In 1939 fewer than four million Americans paid any income tax.[11] Taxes were hiked to pay for the war and for Presidents Herbert Hoover and Franklin Delano Roosevelt's unprecedented rise in domestic spending so that 43 million Americans were paying by 1945.[12] The percentage of families paying the tax rose from about 2 percent to about 65 percent or more. The middle class gasped for breath as the water level of a tax intended to soak the rich sloshed up to its face.

In 1940 Congress added a 10 percent surtax to estate and gift taxes as well as the income tax, largely to prepare for the inevitable day when the United States was blasted into the war enflaming Europe. In 1941 estate tax rates were increased across the board, with the new rates ranging from 3 percent on estates worth less than $40,000 to a record 77 percent on estates worth more than $10 million. The following year, the Revenue Act of 1942 created a $60,000 estate tax exemption and decreased the gift tax exclusions to $30,000 lifetime and $3,000 annual.

In a message to the Congress on April 27, 1942, four months after the United States entered World War II, Roosevelt insisted: "Discrepancies between low personal incomes and very high personal incomes should be lessened . . . I therefore believe that in time of this grave national danger, when all excess income should go to win the war, no American citizen ought to have a net income after he has paid his taxes, of more than $25,000 a year." Thereafter, "[t]o implement the President's proposal, the Treasury . . . recommend[ed] the enactment of a 100 percent war supertax on that part of the net income after regular income tax which exceeds a personal exemption of $25,000."[13]

Explains author Mark Leff:

FDR was a past master at the use of taxation to convey the image of the hour. He explained at one point that he would prefer 'to see a tax which would tax all income above $100,000 at the rate of 99-1/2 percent.' This even shocked his budget director, but the president's joking comeback was revealing one: "Why not? None of us is ever going to make $100,000 a year. How many people report on that much income?" Roosevelt in fact went even further than this. In 1942 and again in 1943, he proposed that all income above $25,000 ($50,000 for families) be taxed away, saying that "all excess income should go to win the war." Inequities, he warned, "seriously affect the morale of soldiers and sailors, farmers and workers, imperiling the efforts to stabilize wages and prices, and thereby impairing the effective prosecution of the war." When this income limit went nowhere in Congress, FDR acted on his own, handing down an executive order limiting after-tax salaries to $25,000 plus certain allowances, only to have his action indignantly repealed by Congress.[14]

Although Congress rescinded Roosevelt's 100 percent income tax rate, tax rates rose again in 1944 — beginning at 23 percent and rising to 94 percent on incomes above $200,000. The tax code's complexity took a harsh toll. Fifty million taxpayers, including 10 million new payers, were baffled by it. There were more complaints to Congress about the complexity of the code than about its astronomical rates. At least one Member understood the complaints. U.S. Representative Robert Doughton, chairman of the tax-writing House Ways and Means Committee, complained that he had to hire a consultant to help him prepare his own income tax. He was better off than Chester Clark, a 42-year-old, unemployed shipbuilder, who committed suicide because he was unable to understand his tax return. He owed $7.50.[15]

The individual income tax had yielded $1.4 billion in 1941, the year the United States entered World War II. When the war ended in 1945, it yielded $19 billion. In 1950, the income tax brought in $17 billion. Also in 1950, the payroll tax rose by one-half to 3 percent and, in 1955, by another one-third to 4 percent. In 1960, payroll taxes were again increased by one-half to 6 percent.[16] Throughout that decade, high tax rates suppressed economy growth.[17]

In 1962, President John F. Kennedy declared, "Our true choice is not between tax reduction on the one hand and the avoidance of large federal deficits on the other. . . . [A]n economy hampered by restrictive tax rates will never produce enough revenues to balance the budget, just as it will never produce enough jobs or enough profits. Surely the lesson of the last decade is that budget deficits are not caused by wild-eyed spenders but by slow economic growth . . ."[18]

Kennedy proposed a series of income tax rate reductions. Legislation the following year reduced the top tax bracket from 91 percent to 70 percent by 1965 and cut taxes by $10 billion. Tax collections from those making more than $50,000 annually soared by 57 percent between 1963 and 1966, while collections from those earning under $50,000 rose by 11 percent. The portion of the federal income tax burden paid by the rich jumped from 11.6 percent to 15.1 percent.[19] Annual federal revenues climbed from $94 billion in 1961 to $150 billion in 1967. Gross national product increased by 10 percent in 1965 and personal income rose by 15 percent in 1966. Unemployment plummeted by nearly one million during the next two years.[20] The Kennedy vigor lived on in a robust U.S. economy.

The Tax Reform Act of 1976 was largely intended to close some of the inevitable loopholes in such a complex system. One of its most significant effects was that it unified estate and gift taxes, with gift taxes assessed according to the same rate schedule as estate taxes. The unified estate and gift tax operates as follows: When a person dies, the government totals all the assets in his estate at their fair market value at the time. Both personal (home, vehicles, and savings) and business (cash, property, equipment) assets are taxed. The government then adds to that total the value of any taxable gifts made during the decedent's lifetime. Then the government subtracts any debts owed against the estate. The tax is assessed on the resulting amount. The new rate structure started at 18 percent for transfers of more than $10,000 and rose to 70 percent for transfers of more than $5 million.[21]

The Act also combined the exemptions for estate and gift taxes into a single unified estate and gift tax credit. The cumulative credit would reduce gift-tax liability during the giver's lifetime. Any balance in the credit left over at death would reduce heirs' estate-tax liability. The credit started at $29,800 for gifts/bequests before 1978 and rose to $46,800 for transfers after 1980. These credit amounts were equivalent to exemptions of $120,000 and $175,000, respectively.[22]

A tax was also added on "generation-skipping transfers," typically bequests granting ownership of property directly to the donor's grandchildren while allowing the donor's children to use the property during their lifetimes, thereby triggerring the estate tax only once—when the estate passed from the first generation to the third—rather than twice— when it passed from the first generation to the second and then again when it passed from the second to the third. The Act also created special rules allowing more small businesses and family farms to escape the tax and raised the marital deduction to $250,000.[23] The ambidextrous grabbing and letting go further complicated an already complex tax.

By the close of the 1970s, the economy suffered both high inflation and high unemployment. (This combination is called "stagflation.") Relief came when President Ronald Reagan cut taxes with the Economic Recovery Tax Act of 1981, also known as the Kemp-Roth Tax Cut. The law slashed income tax rates across the board, lowering the top rate from 70 percent to 50 percent and the bottom from 14 percent to 11 percent. It also indexed tax brackets for inflation, effective in 1985. In addition, the Act lowered the top estate, gift, and generation-skipping transfer tax rates from 70 to 50 percent over three years. It also phased in an increase of the unified estate and gift tax credit from $46,800 to $192,800 (equivalent to exemption amounts of $175,000 and $600,000, respectively). However, the Deficit Reduction Act of 1984 froze the top rate at 55 percent until 1988, instead of letting it drop to 50 percent in 1985. The Omnibus Budget Reconciliation Act of 1987 again delayed the drop in the top estate tax rate until after December 31, 1992.[24]

In 1986 President Reagan pushed through historic tax relief in the form of the the Tax Reform Act of 1986. This Act reduced the number of tax brackets from 15, with a high of 50 percent, to two, of 15 and 28 percent. It also repealed the generation-skipping tax retroactively to June 1, 1976, and replaced it with a flat tax whose rate was equivalent to the top estate tax rate.[25]

In response, personal income tax revenues increased by more than 54 percent between 1983 and 1989 (28 percent after adjusting for inflation).

The portion of income taxes paid by the top 10 percent of earners rose from 48 percent in 1981 to 57.2 percent in 1988. The portion paid by the top 1 percent increased from 17.6 percent to 27.5 percent.[26]

Presidents George Bush and Bill Clinton undermined the progress made by the Reagan cuts with the Omnibus Budget Reconciliation Acts of 1990 and 1993, which added marginal rates of 31, 36, and 39.6 percent. In 1989, individual income tax revenues totaled 8.6 percent of economic output. By 1996, after the Bush and Clinton hikes, revenues from the individual income tax had fallen to 8.5 percent. As The Heritage Foundation's Dan Mitchell points out, "[T]he tax that was increased the most accounts for the drop in tax revenue as a share of national output."[27]

In 1997, Congress passed the Taxpayer Relief Act. This Act increased the unified estate and gift tax credit to $1 million by 2006. It also included a number of pro-family tax cuts, including the child tax credit, educational credits, and capital gains cuts. Regrettably, it greatly exacerbated the complexity of the tax code: it added 36 retroactive changes, 114 changes effective August 5, 1997, 69 changes effective January 1, 1998, and 5 changes effective thereafter, 285 new sections, and 824 amendments.[28]

The Stamp Act crisis set the stage for the Revolutionary War. Despite the mob violence that sometimes accompanied it, colonial resistance to the Stamp Act was fundamentally moral in nature. The colonists objected not so much to the taxes themselves but to the exercise of Parliamentary power and to the precedent established for the future. Suspicious of Parliament, colonial patriots considered its every action in terms of how far it could lead. Thus their outrage over the Stamp Act was not grounded merely in economic considerations but in moral principle. America after the Revolutionary War would have done well to remember the example of its prescient agitators. Perhaps then the damage caused by America's ever-growing burden of taxes could have been averted.

SEVEN

Taxes in the Twenty-First Century

At the dawn of the twenty-first century, the tax burden on Americans was more crushing than ever. In the year 2000, the average American paid 33.6 percent of his income in taxes. By 2009, that figure had dropped to 28.2 percent,[1] thanks largely to President George W. Bush's tax cuts.

President Bush signed a $1.35 trillion tax cut into law in June 2001. The final version of the Economic Growth and Reconciliation Act of 2001 slashed income tax rates across the board, lowering the bottom rate from 15 percent to 10 percent and the top from 39.6 percent to 35 percent. It also eliminates the death tax gradually over ten years.

Regrettably, the Bush cut merely chips at the tax increases of the 1990s and does nothing to reduce the complex structure of the federal tax code, although it at least reverses the rate-raising trend established by the elder President George Bush and continued by President Bill Clinton. In this respect, the younger President Bush began his presidency with a faint yet discernible reflection of the tax-cutting visions of Presidents John F. Kennedy and Ronald Reagan. But just as neither of those two fiscal conservatives was able to return America's tax burden to reasonable size, nor was President Bush.

Overall, the average American family continues to pay more in taxes than for shelter, food, and clothing combined.[2] One way to illustrate Americans' burgeoning tax burden is in terms of how many days each year a person must work just to pay the government. If the typical American began working to pay taxes on January 1 and did not work for himself until all taxes were paid, on what day would he be permitted to keep his own earnings? This date is called Tax Freedom Day, and it has been moving later and later over the last century. In 1913, the year the federal income tax was introduced, Tax Freedom Day was January 30. By 2001, it was May 3.[3] By 2009, it had fallen back a couple of weeks to April 13, thanks mainly to tax cuts and slowing economic growth.[4]

Income Tax

Not surprisingly, the federal income tax is the biggest source of federal revenues and bears the greatest responsibility for Tax Freedom Day's goose-step through the calendar. In 2001, the average American worked 42 days just to pay his individual federal income taxes. He worked an additional 29 days to pay federal social insurance taxes. By contrast, he worked 16 days to pay sales and excise taxes, 15 to pay business taxes, 10 to pay property taxes, and 8 for state and local income taxes.[5] By 2008, the average American worked 32 days — still more than a month — just to pay his individual federal income taxes. He worked an additional 28 days to pay federal social insurance taxes. By contrast, he worked 16 days to pay sales and excise taxes, 13 to pay business taxes, 12 to pay property taxes, and 10 for state and local income taxes.[6]

For tax year 2008, a married couple filing jointly paid 10 percent on the first $16,050 of their taxable income, 15 percent on the remainder up to $65,100, 25 percent on the remainder up to $131,450, 28 percent on the remainder up to $200,300, 33 percent on the remainder up to $357,700, and 35 percent on the rest. This means that, as their incomes rise, families are pushed into higher tax brackets.

A primary objective of President Reagan's historic Tax Reform Act of 1986 — which reduced the number of tax rates from fifteen, with a high of 50 percent; to two, of 15 and 28 percent — was to tax lower- and middle-class Americans at 15 percent, reserving the 28 percent bracket primarily for wealthier taxpayers. Two things have happened to undo the benefits of the Reagan cuts for middle-class families. First came the Bush and Clinton tax increases of the early 1990s, which exacerbated the economic and moral damage caused by a progressive tax system. Second, as incomes have risen, middle-class families have been pushed into the higher brackets.[7]

Payroll taxes

In addition to income taxes, most workers now pay payroll taxes at 15.3 percent, which is split between the employer and employee, hitting the self-employed especially hard. This includes 12.4 percent for Social Security and 2.9 percent for Medicare. Payroll taxes are a greater burden for most workers than are income taxes. Households in the bottom 80 percent of earners filing pay more in Social Security and Medicare payroll taxes (including both employee and employer share) than in income taxes.[8]

As opposed to income taxes, payroll taxes are regressive. Workers begin paying the tax on the first dollar earned with no exemptions or deductions allowed. Income above $106,800 is not subject to Social Security taxes in 2009; although Medicare taxes take 2.9 percent and are assessed on all income with no limit and no deductions or exemptions.

The combination of sharply regressive payroll taxes with progressive income taxes means that middle-class families are subject to the highest marginal federal tax rates. For example, a married couple with $70,000 in taxable wages pays a marginal income tax rate of 25 percent and a payroll tax rate of 15.3 percent, for a total marginal tax rate of 40.3 percent. A taxpayer earning between $600,000 and $6 million pays a marginal rate of 37.9 percent, including the 35 percent income tax and the 2.9 percent Medicare tax. A worker earning $6,000 annually pays no income tax but pays payroll taxes at 15.3 percent. Thus, the middle-income worker is saddled with the highest marginal rate.

Payroll taxes have increased steadily throughout the last century. Of necessity, such will continue to be the case, unless the Social Security system is abolished or fundamentally reformed. This is because more and more revenues will be necessary to pay Social Security benefits. Based upon the Social Security system's own trustees' assumptions, the tax rate needed to fund Social Security in 2045 will range from 17.4 percent to 21.7 percent. When Medicare is added, the rate rises to 31 to 48 percent of workers' incomes.[9] This is in addition to the income and other taxes.

Payroll taxes actually have the bizarre effect of leaving families less able to ensure what they are specifically purported to provide — security in old age. According to The Heritage Foundation, Social Security's inflation-adjusted rate of return is a paltry 1.2 percent for an average household of two 30-year-old earners, each making just under $26,000, with children. This family will pay about $320,000 in Social Security taxes (including their employers' share) and can expect to receive about $450,000 back in payments (1997 dollars, before taxes, assuming that they begin collecting at age 67). Had this typical family allocated the same amount to conservative private investment vehicles, such as traditional individual retirement accounts, they could expect to enjoy a real rate of more than 5 percent per year before taxes, or $975,000 (1997 dollars).[10] Social Security taxes of $320,000 cost this family $525,000.

Estate tax

On the wealth left over after a lifetime of income, payroll, and other taxes, one final tax reaches beyond the grave.

The estate tax in 2009 applies a graduated rate scale that reaches 45 percent, after effectively exempting the first $3,500,000 of the wealth remaining at death. Bequests to a spouse are typically not taxable; a marital deduction effectively exempts most surviving spouses from estate taxation. The gift tax's "annual exclusion amount" is now $13,000, permitting a donor to give up to this amount annually to each of an unlimited number of persons without facing gift taxes.

On January 1, 2010, the death tax is repealed — but only for one year, making repeal of the estate tax a bittersweet and uneasy victory. Moreover, in 2010, the year of the short-lived repeal, assets begin to be inherited at their purchase price rather than their current market value (carryover basis), so heirs inherit old capital-gains liabilities. In other words, while the Bush plan relieves families of one tax, it increases their liability under another. The legislation put the repeal of the death tax on the table, but the back-loading, carryover basis, and sunset clause make this victory less than it appears.

While the estate tax is *de jure* progressive, it is *de facto* regressive. Medium-sized estates actually pay the highest rates. In 1995, estates valued at more than $20 million paid an average tax rate of 12.5 percent, while those valued at $5-20 million paid approximately 17 percent.[11] The most likely medium-sized estate owners are small businesses and family farms.[12] Despite this, some still hail the estate tax as a means to redistribute wealth. "It serves an important social purpose," said Frank Mauro of the Fiscal Policy Institute, a union-funded organization based in New York. "This is an indirect form of income distribution."[13]

The death tax isn't the only vampire rising from the grave to suck the lifeblood from America's economy. A "sunset" provision tacked on in order to move the Bush tax cuts through Congress has stamped an expiration date on the entire tax law. On January 1, 2011, all Bush's celebrated cuts die, and (as of this writing) the nation's tax code is resurrected substantially as it was in 2000. President Bush's tax relief package was better than nothing, but temporary, piecemeal cuts are not enough. America needs fundamental tax reform to undo the damage caused by progressive taxation.

Section III

EIGHT

Destroying Justice in the Name of Fairness

The modern philosophy of government was born during the Progressive era. This philosophy emphasizes a powerful central government that intentionally redistributes wealth. It has largely replaced America's founding philosophy, which emphasized limited government protecting individual rights. The new philosophy has expanded the use of taxation beyond raising revenue in order to "spread the wealth around," in the words of President Barack Obama. Like parents who even out toys to keep their children from quarrelling, civil government uses its power to tax in order to rob Peter and pay Paul. As Shelly Davis, former historian of the IRS says of the progressive income tax, "It was supposed to be a leveler, essentially an unfair tax. It was intended to be a tax on the wealthy."[1] This section explores the effects of modern tax policy. It argues that progressive taxation overturns natural justice and describes the economic and moral damage that twentieth-century tax policy has wrought.

As the Declaration of Independence asserts, civil governments are established to secure rights. They derive the authority to tax from the people in order to fulfill this function. When government begins to tax any person or group for any purpose other than to protect his rights — and especially to violate his rights — it has gone beyond the confines of justice. For the state to take from some of its own citizens, not because they have broken any natural law but simply because they have acquired more than others, is to pervert its own function and to misuse for injustice the power that it has been granted to maintain justice.

Such a perversion of government's proper function has negative effects that go far beyond the injury done to the wealthy minority. Inappropriately expanding the scope of government and confusing its purpose leads citizens to expect more and more of it than they should, enabling it to go on accumulating power while weakening other institutions, such as family, church, and community. It weakens the state's accountability. When the proper functions of government become so blurred to the point that it becomes an instrument of injustice, there is no standard against which to measure expectations and to hold it accountable.

Because Constitutional government has been designed to protect the people from any encroachments of government beyond its proper role, when government ventures to break down natural justice, it necessarily violates the principles of Constitutional justice. This violation assumes many forms.

Equal protection under the law is a hallmark of the Western understanding of justice that culminated in the founding of the United States. Progressive taxation violates this principle. The intent of progressive taxation is to benefit some citizens at the expense of others. In its original form, the modern income tax, like its nineteenth century precursor, was imposed only on a small minority. While this approach partially backfired over the course of the twentieth century and the tax now afflicts the majority of Americans, its discriminatory roots go deep. Though many more now pay some income tax, the code's high marginal rates apply only to some.

Thus the tax code discriminates against some for earning more, imposing a *de facto* fine against citizens who have achieved prosperity for the ostensible benefit of others. This discrimination is frequently defended on the grounds that the so-called rich can afford to pay higher taxes, but justice requires equitable treatment for all, not the selective application of law based on presumed ability to comply.

Civil government undermines its own legitimacy when it imposes law against a specific group. One of the functions of civil government is to protect the rights of a minority against the tyranny of the majority. In the case of discriminatory tax law, the government does the opposite.

Aristotle explained it this way:

[S]uppose the poor use their numerical superiority to make a distribution of the property of the rich: is not that unjust? "No . . ." it may be said, "it has been done justly, by a decision of the sovereign power." [B]ut what else can we call the very height of injustice? . . .

[I]f the majority, having laid their hands on everything, again distribute the possessions of the few, they are obviously destroying the state. . . . [V]irtue does not destroy its possessor, nor is justice destructive of the state. . . . [I]t is clear that this law too cannot be just. . . . [S]econdly, if it *is* just, any actions taken by a tyrant also must be just: his superior strength enables him to use force; just as the mass of people use force on the rich. Thirdly, is it just for the few and the wealthy to rule? If so, and they too do this and plunder and help themselves to the goods of the mass, then that is just. . . . [I]f *that* is so, then it is just in the former case also. The answer clearly is that all these three states of affairs are bad and not just.[2]

As many forewarned early in the history of the income tax, its partiality has led to another of its major injustices: it takes too much money. Having established a toehold by taxing the few at a (relatively, by today's standards) low rate, it was easy and tempting to expand the tax base and increase rates. The resulting tax burden on Americans is more crushing than ever. Part of the problem is that, from the beginning, there have been no checks on the tax code. For example, there are no limits on how much income can be taken, either as a proportion of individual income or of gross domestic product, and only a simple majority vote in Congress is necessary to pass a tax increase.

By acting as an instrument of injustice, progressive taxation robs society of the material benefits of a just order. The twin pillars of wealth creation are private property and free exchange. The virtuous exercise of these rights tends to increase prosperity. When it fulfills its proper function of protecting these rights, civil government fosters economic well-being. But when it abuses its powers in order to violate these rights, government dampens prosperity and spawns economic trouble.

Intended and structured to mitigate the rewards of economic achievement, the U.S. tax system undermines the behavior that promotes the economic growth that strengthens families and the nation. Ironically, it most harms the lower- and middle-class families it was purported to help. As Shelly Davis says of the original creators of the income tax, "They didn't have any idea what they were giving birth to at that time. . . . If they had, they probably would have used birth control."[3]

High marginal rates discourage hard work and entrepreneurship, penalize savings and investment, and destroy jobs. Any tax inevitably discourages whatever is taxed because it raises its cost. This phenomenon is easily observed at every purchase. An item, a book for instance, is marked $30.00, but at the cash register, the buyer is charged $31.50, assuming a 5 percent sales tax. While the extra $1.50 in tax probably isn't enough to keep most people from purchasing the book, consider the added costs of taxation to higher priced goods, like automobiles. The 5 percent sales tax on a $20,000 car is a significant $1,000. This is enough to keep some families from being able to purchase the car, force them to delay buying it, or lure them into assuming added debt.

In 1990, President George Bush imposed a new tax that illustrated the broad negative effects of this phenomenon. Bush's luxury tax was an extra excise applied to five categories of goods: boats costing more than $100,000, cars over $30,000, aircraft over $250,000, and furs and jewels over $5,000. These items were taxed at point of sale at a rate of 10 percent on any amounts above the exempt levels listed above. Predictably, sales of these items declined significantly. This meant that fewer workers were needed to build or design them, and many middle-income earners lost their jobs.

A study by the Republican staff of the Joint Economic Committee found that the luxury tax destroyed at least 9,400 jobs in boat, aircraft, and jewelry manufacturing in 1991 alone.[4] By March of that year, Beech Aircraft Corporation, which sold twice as many private planes as any other company, reported the loss of new retail orders for 39 aircraft worth $77.6 million, costing 255 jobs in that company alone in one year. Spokesman Mike Potts attributed the loss directly to the luxury tax. "We've had (potential buyers) tell us that it's tax-related," he explained.[5]

Though it is less visible, the same phenomenon applies in the case of income taxes. In that case, what is directly discouraged is not purchasing goods but earning income. The discouragement of earning money by working, saving, or investing inherent in any income tax is exacerbated by progressivity. While any high tax rates are economically destructive, high marginal rates are even worse, because high marginal rates particularly discourage productivity and inhibit economic growth. This is because businesses, from small family firms to mega-corporations, lose incentive to grow when growth results in a decreasing return. This disincentive translates into fewer available jobs for workers. Lower job availability also means lower wages for those who find and keep work. Wages are highest when many employers have to compete for few workers; they are lowest when many workers have to compete for few jobs.

It's lower- and middle-class families who suffer most. Wealthy people have choices in these matters. They don't have to produce when productivity stops paying off. Middle- and working-class people do. Although high marginal rates are imposed upon the so-called wealthy, their real costs — fewer jobs, lower wages, slower growth — hit the lower and middle classes the hardest. As Haman was hanged on the gallows he built for Mordecai, so do those who impose high tax rates on others pay the economic costs themselves. When workers succeed despite these obstacles, they're punished with higher tax rates. A progressive tax code unleashes all the wrath on impertinent taxpayers struggling to succeed that Dickens' Mr. Bumble poured on little Oliver Twist, who anticipated their temerity with his legendary cry: "Please, sir, I want some more."

High taxes on savings and investments make these problems even worse. In addition to being high and graduated, taxes on savings and investment are multiplicative. This creates added discouragement of savings and investment, which further diminishes the creation and growth of businesses, available jobs, and wages. It takes middle-class families longer to save the capital needed to start their own businesses. The wealthy are even more discouraged from investment, because their taxes are higher, and so their after-tax return on investment is even lower. This reduces the availability of venture capital from outside sources. Diminishing available capital prevents the creation of new jobs and puts potholes in the would-be entrepreneur's path from a routine job.

By lowering potential pay-off, high investment taxes especially discourage risky investment. Discouragement of risky investment squelches technological advancement, because new technologies are the most risky. This means that our progressive tax system actually reduces progress and inhibits improved quality of life.

The contributions of technological inventors benefit everybody. When an Edison invents the light bulb, a Singer invents the sewing machine, or a Gates invents an operating system, they improve the everyday quality of life of rich and poor alike. It is usually the wealthy who purchase such technology first. This is because newly released technology is necessarily expensive in order to repay the initial costs of research and development and production. Over time, after the first highly priced versions have been purchased and costs met (and the bugs worked out), prices can come down and the product becomes affordable to the majority. Thirty years ago, for example, luxuries like home computers and mobile phones were rare; now almost every household has them.

The notion that the creators and early purchasers of such technology are somehow unjustly wealthy and should be taxed in order to redistribute their wealth is misguided at best. Not only does it ignore the fact that their contributions improve lives, but it even discourages the invention of technology that creates jobs and raises quality of life for everyone.

The irony of envy-based tax policy manifests itself in demagogic opposition to almost every tax cut as "for the rich." It is true that many tax cuts do provide more direct relief for the wealthy, but this is because they pay more taxes in the first place. However, every tax cut benefits the middle class, and many are specifically targeted to the working poor. To oppose tax cuts for these classes just because the rich will benefit too demonstrates the self-defeating nature of public policy based on envy.

Former Vice President Al Gore unwittingly pointed out the absurdity of envy-based tax policy during his speech accepting his party's 2000 nomination to campaign for president of the United States. Gore upheld President Clinton's veto of a tax relief bill with the dubious claim, "[F]or every ten dollars that goes to the wealthiest one percent, middle class families would get one dime. And lower-income families would get one penny."[6]

Thus President Clinton vetoed, with Vice President Gore's approval, tax relief for the lower and middle classes simply because it provided more relief to families paying more in taxes. While Gore's numbers were later shown to be exaggerated, the real problem is his premise that the middle class should not enjoy tax relief if the upper class will benefit as well. The middle and lower classes are not helped when their tax relief is blocked simply because the rich will benefit too; they are helped by any tax relief, especially across-the-board relief that directly lowers their taxes and stimulates the growth that creates more jobs and increases wages.

Cuts in investment taxes have long been derided as tax cuts for the rich. In the past, the argument was merely superficial. Until recently, it was primarily the rich who invested, but the fruits of their investment paid off in greater economic growth, more jobs, and higher wages that benefit the middle and lower classes. To argue that investment taxes hit only the rich is to ignore the benefits of economic growth to all Americans.

Lately, thanks to the dramatic increase in middle-class investors, even this superficial argument has lost what little credence it once had. In 1935, 68.7 percent of "prosperous" and 33.5 percent of "upper middle class" households owned securities, while only 14.9 percent of "lower middle class" and 2.9 percent of "poor" households did so.[7] By 1995, 50 percent of stockholding families earned $50,000 or less.[8] These families' investment earnings, intended for future financial security, education, or health emergencies, are diminished by our punitive tax policies. The rise of the new investor class has meant that investment taxes, far from affecting only the rich, have shifted from merely injuring middle-class families indirectly to injuring them directly as well.

The tax-the-rich scheme that is most harmful to the middle class is the estate tax. According to Kristin Hogarth of the National Federation of Independent Business (NFIB), the average family business spends about $20,000 annually in legal fees, nearly $12,000 in accounting fees, and $11,000 for estate tax planning advisors.[9] The $43,000 sum of these annual costs could be used to provide a job. A survey of 365 family-owned businesses in New York found that each had spent an average of $125,000 on estate planning. The resultant cuts in labor and investment reduced employment by more than 5,000 jobs.[10] Adam Smith foresaw such job destruction in 1776, when he wrote, "All taxes upon the transference of property of every kind, so far as they diminish the capital value of that property, tend to diminish the funds destined for the maintenance of productive labor."[11]

According to the president of the 60 Plus Association, James L. Martin, nearly 90 percent of family-owned businesses do not survive past a second generation. They are forced to sell off assets to pay the death tax because the paper value of the farm or business greatly exceeds the death-tax exemption level.[12] This is because these enterprises have typically reinvested most of their earnings back into the business, for example by purchasing equipment or hiring staff. While this is often the only way to keep small businesses afloat, it inflates the enterprise's on-paper value, raising its tax liability, but leaves it little in the way of cash reserves with which to pay the taxes.

Because of the Constitutional and practical harm that progressive taxation causes, the tax code is frequently changed. Regrettably, these changes only address the symptoms of progressivity and are almost never implemented with any regard to rational principles or their likely consequences. For example, in order to mitigate some of the damage caused by high marginal rates, the tax code allows myriad exemptions, deductions, and credits. (Ironically, these preferences themselves are subject to income limits, meaning that they lose value for the people most injured by high marginal rates.)

Though they are imposed in order to mitigate the negative effects of the tax code without altering the basic structure that produces these effects, many would-be reforms actually worsen the tax nightmare. One example of this phenomenon is a provision known as the alternative minimum tax (AMT), which requires some taxpayers to calculate their taxes twice according to two different methods and then pay whichever tax bill is larger.

The AMT operates as follows under current law: First, taxpayers calculate their taxes using the normal procedure. Then many must also complete an IRS worksheet to determine whether they might have to pay the AMT; the higher their deductions and credits, the more likely they are to be subject to it. To find out for sure, they must complete another IRS form requiring them to add back to their taxable income a long list of so-called tax preferences, including deductions for state and local taxes, charitable contributions, and even the standard deduction and personal exemptions.

Next, they subtract an AMT exemption, the exact amount of which decreases as income rises. The full exemption amount is $45,000 for joint returns and $33,750 for single returns; it phases out at a rate of 25 cents for every dollar of AMT income above $150,000 for joint returns and $112,500 for single returns. Then they calculate their taxes again—this time using their revised taxable income and different AMT tax rates. Finally, they compare their tax bill under the normal procedure with their liability under the AMT procedure—and pay whichever amount is larger.

The AMT was first imposed in 1969 in response to a Treasury Department study that reported that 155 individuals making more than $200,000 ($875,000 in 1997 dollars) had faced no federal income tax liability in 1967.[13] This was because our complicated tax structure enabled them to escape liability. Outraged, Congress altered the tax structure in order to ensure that all upper-income citizens pay federal income taxes, even when legitimate deductions and credits would otherwise eliminate their liability.

The first version of the AMT, which took effect in 1970, was actually a 10 percent add-on tax, meaning that it was paid in addition to regular tax liability. In 1978, a new version of the AMT, paid instead of regular tax liability, was added. Its graduated rates ranged from 10 to 25 percent. The Tax Equity and Fiscal Responsibility Act of 1982 eliminated the add-on tax and greatly expanded the AMT. This revised AMT imposed a flat rate of 20 percent, which was later increased to 21 percent under the Tax Reform Act of 1986. The Revenue Reconciliation Act of 1993 again graduated the AMT, with rates of 26 and 28 percent.[14]

Unlike the regular income tax, the AMT is not indexed for inflation. This guarantees annual tax increases for millions of Americans. Because of this, forty years after its first version was imposed, growing numbers of middle-class families are subject to the alternative minimum tax. If it is not changed, approximately one in four income taxpayers will be subject to the AMT by 2013.[15] The self-defeating irony of envy-based tax policy is perhaps best illuminated by this one ludicrous phenomenon: A provision seeking to force 155 wealthy people in 1970 to pay income taxes annually causes millions of middle-class families to pay higher taxes.

The AMT in all its complexity is a microcosm of our overall tax code. According to Nina Olson, national taxpayer advance at the I.R.S., "[T]he tax code has grown so long that it's challenging to figure out its length."[16]

The complexity of the tax code makes compliance very expensive. The Tax Foundation estimated that the costs of complying with the tax code totaled $140 billion in 2001.[17] Compliance costs refer to the costs of obeying the law, e.g., keeping records, purchasing tax software, employing tax lawyers and accountants. Compliance costs matter because they are a drain on the economy. They don't increase wealth, and they divert money from activities that could. For example, when a citizen pays an accountant to prepare his tax return, he receives nothing tangible in return. By contrast, when he pays a builder to build a house, he gets a house. That house is wealth; a completed tax return isn't, and it has consumed financial resources that could have been used on the house or another asset.

Complexity endangers the republican form of government. Inherent to a republic or representative democracy is the idea of citizens granting consent to the laws that govern them through their elected representatives.

In practice, this consent of the governed is kneecapped by the complexity of the tax code. The Internal Revenue Code disproportionately expands the power of the tax-writing committees of Congress, whose members are courted by special interest lobbyists. The tax loopholes created in response to this lobbying empower Members of Congress by deceiving taxpayers. Former Senator Malcolm Wallop (R-Wyoming) provides an example of how this happens:

> Tuition tax credits are another wonder. Of course, tax preferences are responsible for the education of the children of the hard-pressed middle class, are they not? Yet statistics show that one of the reasons college tuition outpaces inflation derives specifically from higher education's skill at becoming a principal beneficiary of government favors. The parents run in place while increased tuition costs absorb their promised relief.
>
> This may not be a direct form of corruption, but it is an exercise of power to obtain political credit without identifying the cost. Its intent is to deceive the taxpayer. To that extent, it is a temptation to elected officials who publicly decry tax loopholes and added complication but apply the former and expand the latter without hesitation and without political blame.[18]

Perhaps even less transparent is the power delegated by default to unelected staff members. Senator Wallop relates the following story:

> Senator Cliff Hansen, my predecessor on the Senate Finance Committee, told me how a $500,000 cap on the exemption for agricultural estate taxes came to be. In a 1978 tax bill, Senator Hansen asked Senator Abe Ribicoff to join him in providing relief from estate taxes to farmers and ranchers who stayed on their land for ten years after the death of the parent. Senator Ribicoff liked the idea and said he would join if Hansen would expand it to include small business proprietors as well. It passed unanimously in the committee and handsomely in the Senate.
>
> When they got to conference, however, the two Senators were surprised to see that the amount that could be passed on to the children without being double-taxed had been capped at $1 million.

[When both the Senate and the House pass legislation, it has frequently been changed in different ways in each house, resulting in different bills. Members from both houses then meet to iron out the differences and create one bill. This arrangement is called a Conference Committee.] They asked Chairman Russell Long where the cap had come from, and he said he didn't know. . . . [U]pon inquiring, Long discovered that his staff director had inserted it on his own because *he* didn't think it was appropriate uncapped [emphasis in original]. The House had no similar provision, so the compromise cut the amount in half.[19]

This wasn't much of a compromise. It made things worse. The compromise between a cap and no cap is a higher cap, not a lower one. This case is but another argument for keeping the tax code—and all law—simple, for when it becomes too unwieldy for the people's elected representatives to keep track of what they're voting on, things that they never intended are bound to creep in. This absurd scenario illustrates how far the United States has strayed from the accountable republic she was founded to be. When unelected staffers are making incomprehensible law even more so, there is no "consent of the governed."

Perhaps the most immediate injustice of tax complexity is that it makes it impossible for the well-meaning citizen to rest secure in the knowledge that he has not violated the law. In June 1997, the National Commission on Reform of the IRS, which Congress had appointed to study the issue, reported that the complex structure of the tax code placed a severe burden on honest citizens seeking to comply.

It is fundamental to the western concept of justice that citizens be aware of the laws to which they are subject. The tax code does violence to this fundamental basis of law and to America's own philosophical heritage.

The dangers of this absurd complexity are annually illustrated by *Money* magazine. Every year, the magazine conducts an experiment asking a number of tax professionals to calculate a hypothetical family's taxes. Almost every year, no two tax experts come up with the same answer. This result is largely due to the incomprehensibility of a tax code so complicated that even professional preparers can't agree on what it means. For example, two certified public accountants who vetted *Money*'s 1998 test for accuracy couldn't agree on a specific aspect of the tax treatment of rental property.

One argued that the expenses on such property were no longer deductible once the tenants vacated; the other "argued just as persuasively that the expenses were deductible until the property was sold."[20]

If professional tax preparers can't figure taxes correctly, how can the average family? Families are forced to spend hours slogging through the tax code's morass of minutiae or sacrifice hard-earned money to pay someone else to calculate their taxes for them, but even then they can't be sure that their tax returns are being prepared correctly.

This is especially injurious to middle-income taxpayers. While the wealthy can afford high-priced accountants and lawyers to tread through the tax labyrinth for them, finding the hidden legal ways to lower their tax bills, middle-class families cannot.

Wealthy Americans can pay professionals to help them avoid higher tax bills. Commenting on tax-the-rich schemes, Thomas J. Stanley, a market researcher who studies the affluent says, "[T]he people in government have grossly underestimated the intellect of these people. . . . They are extremely clever. They are not going to let a group of bureaucrats take their money from them. They have an array of high-paid tax consultants who will minimize the impact."[21] Middle-class families often don't have this option, and they cannot even rely on guidance from the IRS, which frequently gives taxpayers the wrong information about their returns. Humorist Dave Barry wrote that tax laws "are constantly changing as our elected representatives seek new ways to ensure that whatever tax advice we receive is incorrect."[22]

Unsurprisingly, this unjust system is enforced by means outside the confines of justice and without respect for taxpayers' privacy. The nature of any income tax will be to violate privacy. This is especially true of one that is impossibly complex and enforced by an unaccountable agency.

Protection of privacy was among the main motivations for the Revolutionary War. The Writs of Assistance issued by the British government and the forcible quartering of British troops in family homes were privacy issues. These measures subjected the colonists to unjustified state intrusion.

In the same way, the income tax is a privacy issue. Complying with the income tax requires citizens to report to the federal government their income, its sources, and what they spend it on. This is information that people don't give even their closest friends. Such information turns government from servant to overlord, entitled to know the most intimate details of people's lives. It teaches that government is an intimate and that the state is in some way closer than a friend. It accustoms citizens to federal invasiveness and pushes back the boundaries of authority.

By violating the sanctity of the privacy of any unconvicted person from government inspection, the income tax weakens all against further federal intrusion. This point was driven home in 1995 when the IRS inaugurated "economic reality audits" designed to "audit the taxpayer, not just the tax return," according to the agency's then-Commissioner Margaret Richardson. Dubbed Calvin Klein audits "because the IRS agent practically goes through a person's closet to see how expensive his jeans are," these lifestyle audits were intended to catch tax cheaters by finding citizens whose lifestyles appear beyond their reported incomes. Agents inquired about cash on hand, the health of the taxpayer and his family, and the sources of funding for their education. According to Kay Howard, project manager for the Economic Reality Training program, everything that "goes on with a taxpayer's income is within the scope of an audit."[23] The premise of this arrogant notion is that the civil government is entitled to know every detail of a taxpayer's spending, which is tantamount to knowing every detail of his life. This undermines the citizen's liberty at the most fundamental level, leaving no aspect of his life beyond the snooping eye of the state.

As James Otis said of the Writs of Assistance more than 200 years ago, "It is a power, that places the liberty of every man in the hands of every petty officer."[24] As the colonists recognized, to submit to such invasion of privacy in tax matters is to invite it in all other matters. Once the moral argument that civil government has no authority to invade privacy in any one facet of life has been dismissed, it must logically be dismissed in all other facets.

Taxpayer abuse by the IRS is well documented. The IRS is known to be Draconian in its enforcement of the tax laws that even it cannot understand and is not constrained by the demands of due process.

The IRS, for instance, enjoys the power to search Americans' financial records without warrants and to seize their property without trial. This means that innocent taxpayers are less secure in their rights than murderers, rapists, and thieves. These criminals are protected from searches without warrants and property seizure before conviction; no such protections exist for the taxpayers, be they errant or innocent. According to the Government Accountability Office (GAO), the IRS makes unjustified seizures of the paychecks and bank accounts of tens of thousands of citizens and businesses annually.[25]

A 1997 Senate Finance Committee investigation found that:

- The agency prefers to audit middle- and low-income taxpayers. These are the taxpayers least likely to be able to afford protracted legal battles.
- Tax assessments that have no basis in fact or tax law were levied simply to "raise the individual statistics of an IRS employee."
- The use of collection quotas to rate the success of agents or officers, prohibited in a 1988 law, is commonplace. Using dollar quotas instead of other criteria, such as accuracy or respectful treatment of citizens, encourages tax collectors to press for amounts that are not legally due.
- Many revenue officers were issued false identification, in violation of IRS rules, making them unaccountable, according to Committee Chairman William V. Roth, Jr. (R-Del.).[26]

According to Roth,

Our six month long look at the IRS shows a troubled agency, with widespread, serious problems. At a minimum, the cases brought to our attention paint a picture of an unresponsive agency with some employees who do not care about the taxpayers they serve. At the worst, our investigation has uncovered an agency in which a subculture of fear and intimidation has been allowed to flourish — both in the internal treatment of some employees, and in the treatment of some taxpayers.[27]

His view is borne out by reports from inside the agency itself. For example, a district manager in Los Angeles posted on his door a sign that read: "Seizure Fever — Catch It."[28] A retired revenue officer related a threat from his boss in testimony before a Congressional subcommittee: "He said that if he was removed because of low production and low seizure activity, he was going to take a lot of people with him."[29]

"Seizure fever" is especially disturbing given the agency's carelessness with the returns of compliant taxpayers. In 1985, IRS Commissioner Roscoe Egger admitted to a "serious breakdown" and apologized to taxpayers. IRS employees had deliberately destroyed citizens' tax documents and returns. Dozens of unprocessed returns and payments totaling hundreds of thousands of dollars were found in a trash barrel outside the IRS service center in northeast Philadelphia. In all, hundreds of thousands of tax returns were lost; millions piled up in IRS processing centers; refunds worth hundreds of millions of dollars were delayed or incorrect; fully compliant taxpayers received dunning notices and threats to seize property.[30]

In addition to violating citizens' rights, IRS persecution of tax evaders and alleged evaders as criminals turns justice on its head by treating such an offense on the same level with violation of another's rights.

Adam Smith held that a typical tax evader "would have been, in every respect, an excellent citizen, had not the laws of his country made that a crime which nature never meant to be so."[31]

Baron de Montesquieu, the French jurist and political philosopher on whose theory of separation of powers the American founders relied, agreed. Arguing that tax evasion was the consequence of excessive rates, he wrote: "Recourse must, therefore, be had to extravagant punishments, such as those inflicted for capital crimes. All proportion then of penalties is at an end. Persons that cannot really be considered as vicious men are punished like the most infamous criminals, which of all things in the world, is the most contrary to the spirit of a moderate government."[32]

Sir William Blackstone, the British jurist and legal scholar whose *Commentaries on the Laws of England* was used for more than a century as the foundation of all legal education in Britain and the United States, echoed the point, explaining that treating tax evasion as a criminal offense is dangerous because it "destroys all proportion of punishment, and puts murderers upon equal footing with such as are really guilty of no natural, but merely a positive offence."[33]

The arrogance that would treat keeping the fruits of one's own labor on par with murder reveals the tendency of government to view itself as holder of rights of its own, rather than protector of the rights of its citizens. It shows contempt for the centuries of developing thought of the ideas of justice and the proper functions of government that contribute to the philosophical basis of America's founding.

The actual stories of broken families, destroyed businesses, and suicides attest to the danger of allowing this perception to fester. One night in 1988, Kay Council returned home to find a suicide note from her husband Alex, who wrote:

> My dearest Kay: I have taken my life in order to provide capital for you. The I.R.S. and its liens which have been taken against our property illegally by a runaway agency of our government have dried up all sources of credit for us. So I have made the only decision I can. It's purely a business decision. I hope you can understand that.
>
> I love you completely. Alex.

Alex Council shot himself in the head.[34]

A revenue officer in Philadelphia laughed about telling a mother who had no income and no means to pay her alleged tax debt, "If you can't pay your taxes, then bring your kids in and we'll sell them for you."[35] A pregnant woman whose husband was jumped and handcuffed by a self-identified U.S. marshal and a group of IRS agents gave birth prematurely eight days later to twins, one of whom died. She reports that her pregnancy had been normal before the attack and that one of the officers involved was promoted for using "fear tactics."[36]

In response to outrage over episodes like this, Congress passed the IRS Reform and Restructuring Act in 1998, designed to quell these abuses. The Act included a taxpayers' bill of rights that included shifting the burden of proof in court cases from the taxpayer to the IRS, protecting citizens from prosecution and punishment for tax crimes committed by their spouses, disallowing the agency to seize primary residences to settle tax debt, allowing wronged taxpayers to recover punitive damages, and demanding the termination of abusive audit agents. The law also mandates that Congress issue a report analyzing the impact of every new tax bill on the code's complexity and that an oversight board be appointed.

Results of the legislation have been mixed at best. IRS data show that the as of August 2000, agency fired only four of its sixteen thousand auditors for improperly threatening audits. One case involved an auditor, who was arrested for driving while intoxicated, telling a police officer that he would "find out" about him and have "a good time" with him.[37] The threat is eerily reminiscent of an episode recounted by James Otis in his famous speech, "A man's house is his castle:"

> Mr. Justice Walley had called . . . Mr. Ware before him by a constable, to answer for a breach of Sabbath-day acts, or that of profane swearing. As soon as he had finished, Mr. Ware [over to whom a Writ of Assistance had been endorsed] asked him if he had done. He replied, Yes. "Well then," said Mr. Ware, "I will show you a little of my power. I command you to permit me to search your house for uncustomed goods." And went on to search his house from the garret to the cellar; and then served the constable in the same manner.[38]

Nearly two years after passage, Senator Roth told the Senate Finance Committee:

> Many of the egregious practices of the past continue. Enforcement statistics are still illegally being used in the IRS, which, as this Committee revealed, may result in violation of taxpayers' rights. Over 46,000 innocent spouse claims have yet to be resolved. In many cases, taxpayers are not being afforded due process. The use of liens and seizures has plummeted, yet the I.R.S. does not follow the law or its procedures a third of the time when it actually issues a lien or [s]eizes property. . . .[39]

The National Taxpayers Union (NTU) estimated that complaints of agent abuse declined by only one-third, and the Union found no decrease in the number of bureaucratic errors, e.g. situations where a data entry error results in a taxpayer being incorrectly assessed a high tax bill and receiving numbers of dunning notices. While the agency has expanded customer service hours and improved access via its 800-number, the accuracy of advice given over the telephone to taxpayers has actually declined. While taxpayers are no longer held criminally liable for following the agency's wrong advice, they are financially liable for paying interest that accrues. Two years after the oversight board was to meet, it had not even been formed.[40] A report issued in August 2000 by the Congressional Joint Committee on Taxation disclosed that none of the 830 complaints filed by taxpayers under the new law had been upheld.[41]

As Terry Little, an IRS employee and president of the Denver National Treasury Employees Union (NTEU), which represents I.R.S. workers, explains, "From the employee's standpoint, it's a little bit difficult to deal with change this fast. . . . In the past Congress kind of wanted us to be the pit bulls, so to speak, and unfortunately we may have been too much of one. It's hard to change overnight."[42]

Agitation for repeal of the law began quickly. Colleen Kelley, president of the NTEU insisted, "The law fixes a problem that doesn't exist."[43] Others claim that it actually creates problems, like declining revenues. Some argue that Congress should repeal the law in order to protect revenues. Labeling the 1997 Congressional hearings on agency abuse an "IRS witch hunt," self-described IRS employee John Kelshaw wrote in a letter to the editor of the *Asbury Park Press*:

> This law was so stringent that it forced IRS employees to stop doing their jobs of enforcing the tax laws and collecting the proper tax for fear of losing their jobs. Now, the agency has basically one focus: customer service. What is the result? Fewer audits and less money coming into the government's coffers. Since we do not have the resources or time to audit the returns with high adjustment potential, we turn to the "smaller returns." Why? Because it doesn't take as much time and it is easier because, generally, all of their income and expenses (taxes, mortgage interest, etc.) are reported to the IRS via a paper document (W-2, 1099).
>
> Since the IRS brings in roughly 90–95 percent of all government funding, how long will it be before Congress members get upset that there is no money for their pork-barrel projects? Congress enacts the laws and then directs IRS employees to enforce them, but then threatens to fire employees if they try to enforce the laws and complains when work doesn't get done because the employees are afraid of getting fired. Sound confusing and hypocritical? You're right.[44]

While the symbolic importance of IRS reform should not be ignored, such legislation alone cannot reform the agency. The arrogance of the IRS reveals its contempt for the rights, even the humanity, of the citizens whom it allegedly serves. The problem is deeper than a runaway federal agency and cannot be fully eradicated by legislation, no matter how necessary or well intended.

It is foolish to expect justice in the enforcement of unjust law. As Lord Acton warned, "Power tends to corrupt, and absolute power corrupts absolutely." Almost everyone is susceptible to the intoxication of power. Those who choose the enforcement of an unjust system as a career are likely to be among the most susceptible, for they are not morally constrained by the demands of justice. IRS auditors are people who deliberately choose work enforcing a discriminatory system. They ask strangers invasive questions in adversarial contexts intended to yield more of these strangers' money. Aggressiveness, intimidation, and threats bring greater success. To expect legislation to resolve this fully is naïve.

When government misuses fiscal policy to pick winners and losers it reduces self-government to a divisive struggle between groups seeking to advance their perceived special interests instead of a unifying quest for the common good found in the natural order.

This encourages citizens to view one another as adversaries and en-courages political decision-making on the basis of perceived self-interest rather than impartial justice. Votes are sought and cast not on the basis of what is just and beneficial to the nation as a whole but rather on the basis of what the voter believes to be in his own immediate self-interest without regard for the rights of others.

When a government does to people not convicted of any wrongdoing what the people cannot do to one another, the march toward tyranny has begun. When it takes from some just because they have more than others, when it places its interests in self-support above the privacy of its citizens, when its enforcement of an unnatural law is identical to its enforcement of heinous natural offences, when it can't even understand its own laws, it has shifted from enforcing justice to enforcing injustice and sows dis-respect for the Rule of Law. It becomes an instrument of the very wrongs it is instituted to subdue.

NINE

Taxing Virtue

Progressive taxation is a clever con artist. It promises to pay society's toll on the road toward utopia, where every family's finances are above average. But its promises are false. And while it's making these false promises, progressive taxation is subtly appealing to the vices that plague human nature. Its lofty, noble-sounding promises provide cover for its real aim: robbing individuals, families, and society as a whole of their well-being by discouraging virtue and affirming vice. While promising a greater good, progressive taxation fools people into giving up what leads to economic and moral prosperity.

The progressive tax system is based on envy, the "resentful awareness of an advantage enjoyed by another joined with a desire to possess the same advantage."[1] As earlier chapters have explained, the modern U.S. tax code was imposed in response to so-called progressives agitating against the natural inequality in wealth distribution. Basing public policy on envy teaches people to nurture their natural tendency toward this vice, instead of to resist and rise above it. It encourages everyone to think himself a victim and perpetuates resentment because there will always be something to envy.

At the same time that it validates this vice, progressive taxation discourages the virtuous behavior that creates wealth, such as work and saving. That means that it also discourages the discipline that these things require. By diminishing the likelihood of prosperity and its endurance, progressive taxation obscures the importance of vision, forethought, and careful planning needed to achieve it. By making immediate consumption cheaper than saving, it discourages sacrifice and delayed gratification. This discouragement affirms the human temptation to seek immediate desires over long-term good. The urgent and absolute nature of tax planning decisions blunts the exercise of wisdom, reason, and discernment by forcing people into sub-optimal decisions. By seizing the fruits of hard work, tenacity, and facing challenge, progressive taxation encourages laziness. As these attitudes insinuate themselves into the culture, people become less disciplined and more easily swayed by immediate desires.

Because it discourages people from pursuing virtue, progressive taxation also robs both individuals and society as a whole of its benefits. Virtue carries natural rewards, often including prosperity. Hard work refines people by requiring discipline and building character. Work keeps people active, sharpens their minds, and provides fulfillment. To discourage it means to discourage people from improving themselves, from contributing all that they can to their families and communities, and from pushing their own limitations.

Virtue brings other benefits, such as greater freedom from worry, self-respect, and the trust and confidence of others. Virtues become habits when practiced regularly, building healthy families, healthy communities, and healthy nations. While virtue is not a guarantee against hardship, people are almost universally better positioned to meet difficult times if they have developed strong character, built their nest eggs, and established good reputations. A nation that treats the fruits of virtue as sinister is a nation in moral peril because it lures its citizens away from the behaviors that promote moral well-being.

Progressive taxation also corrodes the family, one of the institutions responsible for inculcating virtue. That's partly because of what has come to be called the "marriage penalty," a consequence of the progressive tax structure that requires some couples to pay higher taxes simply because they're married.

The marriage penalty, or marriage tax, is the amount that a married couple pays in income taxes beyond what they would pay if they were not married. In 1996, 21 million American families paid an average of nearly $1,400 in marriage penalties, according to a major study conducted by the Congressional Budget Office.[2] According to another estimate, this means that an average couple married forty years would pay an extra $56,000 in marriage taxes.[3]

The progressive tax structure is the primary cause of the marriage penalty. Tax units with higher incomes are taxed at higher rates and lose eligibility for credits and deductions. (A tax unit is the entity taxed — either an individual or a married couple.) Since marriage combines two tax units into one, a married couple's combined income can mean that their joint tax liability is higher than the sum of what their individual tax bills as single filers would be.

The marriage penalty violates the very essence of what America stands for. Equality under the law is a fundamental American ideal. By treating married couples inequitably, the tax code makes a mockery of this ideal.

The marriage penalty imposes specific social costs as well. By discriminating against married couples, the tax code discourages marriage. Economists James Alm and Leslie Whittington found that the probability of marriage falls as the marriage tax rises.[4] One consequence of the increasing likelihood of couples eschewing marriage is an increase in non-marital cohabitation. In 1960, fewer than 500,000 unmarried couples lived together. By 1997 that number was more than 4 million.[5] This has helped normalize extramarital sexual relations, the damaging social effects of which are well documented.

There is enough anecdotal evidence to demonstrate that at least some of this increase is due to the marriage penalty. Testifying before the Ways and Means Committee, Sharon Mallory, a forty-one-year-old factory worker from Indiana, said that she and her live-in companion, Darryl Pierce, wanted to marry but couldn't afford the $3,700 in additional taxes. "Darryl and I love each other very much and want to be married," Ms. Mallory testified. "[T]he IRS won't let us. We're victims of the marriage penalty."[6]

Echoing Ms. Mallory, Robin Blumner, a columnist and editorial writer for the *St. Petersburg Times*, wrote that she and her boyfriend lived together for seven years "without benefit of marriage. We own a house together with rights of survivorship and we are beneficiaries of each other's life insurance. (My parents call him their sin-in-law.) For all intents and purposes, we are married — just without the license. And more importantly, without the tax liability. An accountant figured out that our yearly tax bill would go up by nearly $1,000 if we said 'I do.' Which means, as to marriage, we don't."[7]

Of course, cohabitation would not be such a common choice if not for growing social acceptance of it, yet, conversely, behaviors become socially accepted because large numbers of people start exhibiting them. Cohabitation has risen along with mounting violations against the sanctity of marriage and the rejection of traditional religion and its moral teachings. While not alone in creating such an environment, anti-marriage tax policy joins with these other social forces in perpetuating it.

Instead of deciding against marriage altogether, some couples postpone it until a later tax year.[8] This delay denigrates marriage by forcing it to accommodate the tax code. For those who do marry, the extra tax burden reduces the economic freedom to meet family needs. The Congressional Budget Office's estimated average annual marriage tax of $1,400 could cover, for example, a couple of mortgage payments, a down payment on a car, or a vacation, or it could be saved or invested to earn interest or dividends. For poorer families, the marriage tax can present an issue of financial survival. Consider what one newly married woman wrote to Family Research Council:

> When I became a Christian, about two years ago, my [now-]husband and I discussed getting married . . . to be faithful to God. I never really knew what we were getting ourselves into until we did our 1999 income taxes. I know we are just one of the millions of couples experiencing the consequences of the Marriage Penalty.
>
> My husband and I have both been single parents for quite a long time prior to this. We both received a refund every year. Not that much, but we never had to pay and never dreamed of it, living on the income that we share. . . . We live in a small, very simple home, have one car payment . . . and the regular utilities. We don't have extra expenses such as comput[e]rs, pets, cell phones, steak[;] in fact paper towels are a luxury.
>
> To say the least, we were both in shock when we had our taxes done this year and were told we owed over $1600.00. We don't even have a savings account. We gathered together [$]400.00 to pay to Federal and [$]435.00 for State. . . . We don't know how we are going to pay for this before year[']s end. We were so upset for days, tossing around ideas prior to next year.
>
> We discussed getting divorced, moving into an apartment and renting out our home. Renting out our upstairs and reducing our living space was also an option. None of these were at all appealing to us. My next thought is to go to our local I.R.S. office and say we just don't have it and pray . . . for the best.

We are probably considered lower middle class but soon we will be pushed into poverty. Will we have to sell some of our belongings to keep afloat[?] What happens when we run out of things to sell[?][9]

Sad as it is, the damage done to struggling families like these is only part of the marriage tax's deleterious social effects. By leaving cohabiting couples with more disposable income than married couples, the tax code gives the former more influence over the culture. This influence shows up in books, music, movies, and television programs that popularize illicit sex and denigrate family values.

By making marriage more expensive than non-marriage, the tax code also creates strong incentives to divorce. Whittington and Alm have found significant response to these incentives, particularly among women.[10]

The most celebrated couple to divorce because of the marriage tax was Angela and David Boyter. Until the government stopped the practice, the Boyters used to divorce late every year and then remarry early the next year simply so that they could each claim single filing status and save themselves tax dollars. They often paid for vacations with their tax savings.[11] While this behavior is extreme, it highlights the absurd fact that the tax code actually rewards divorce. More often, according to divorce lawyer John Crouch, the marriage penalty drives separated couples to file for divorce and to complete their divorces as quickly as possible. This discourages reconciliation attempts and destroys marriages that might have been saved.[12]

Even single-income families, who appear not to pay marriage penalties, are presented by the tax code with an incentive to divorce. Normally when such a couple divorces, income is transferred from the wage earner to the non-earner in the form of alimony. In these cases, the couple's overall tax bill can be reduced as the earner's tax bracket is lowered by transferring income to the non-earner.[13] Thus, a single-income couple could actually reduce their combined tax bill by divorcing and shifting income from one spouse to the other.

With its incentives to reject or postpone marriage, to cohabit, and to divorce, the tax code robs society of the benefits of strong families while encouraging more of the problems caused by family breakdown. This, in turn, increases demands for expensive government programming to address social problems — which, of course, increases the demand for taxes.

Progressive taxation also harms the family by limiting personal and familial freedom. First, it directly limits disposable income, seizing honest earnings. Second, it reduces the number of available jobs and lowers the wages of the jobs that remain. Third, it increases the difficulties of entrepreneurship and possibilities of failure, undermining the success of small businesses. The effects of this encroachment are not merely economic; those are only the most obvious ones. People have specific moral responsibilities, including providing for themselves and their families, both their children and their parents in the proper course of time, and giving to their churches and to charities. The more government takes from them, the less they have with which to meet these moral responsibilities. Anything that diminishes economic freedom consequently diminishes moral freedom, the freedom to do what one ought.

The burden that this interference places on families was eloquently summed up by full-time mom and former schoolteacher Susie Dutcher before the U.S. Senate Finance Committee on April 22, 1998:

> Taxes are far and away the biggest portion of our family budget. There are many things I would like to do with my husband's earnings, but ... you seem to believe you have the moral authority and the superior judgment to make those choices for us. I would love to put more dollars into our retirement account, for example, but I'm forced to put them into your Social Security trust fund, which I don't trust. I'd love to buy more books for Lincoln, Elizabeth, and Mary Margaret and put more money in their college fund, but you've already seen fit to use that money funding closed-captioning for the "Jerry Springer" show. I'd love to get ballet lessons for Elizabeth, but my money is tied up buying food stamps for the deceased. I'd love to give more money to support our church's missionary in Albania ... but instead I'm forced to fund fish farming ... and Social Security disability payments for escaped convicts. My husband and I would like for the most part to make our own choices concerning the fruit of our labor. But under threat of imprisonment, we defer to your choices.[14]

Punitive levels of taxation restrict families' freedom to meet their moral responsibilities. An ever-heavier tax burden forces families to sacrifice time together, forgo essential and non-essential goods and services, and accept lower quality in those goods and services. For many families, the high cost of taxation means that both parents must work outside the home for pay and leave their children in the care of others. Many more forgo educating their children at the best schools. Many are cost necessary luxuries, like a second car or a family vacation and the precious time together that it would allow.

Education provides a case in point. Taxpayers send their money to three levels of government to be returned in the form of public education for the nation's children. As a result, many financially strapped middle-income families lose the freedom to send their children to private schools where they may be better off. Any number of factors could be considered in determining the best educational environment for one's child. Does the school's religious foundation or moral code reflect — or at least respect — the family's? Is the curriculum suited to the child's needs and interests? Does the school offer a particular extra-curricular activity that would help the child develop a certain talent? Is its disciplinary ethic appropriately strict or flexible to meet the child's needs? Does it send a permissive message through explicit sex education and/or condom distribution?

It is at the heart of parental responsibility to provide the best education for one's children. To the degree that taxation restricts parents' economic freedom to fulfill this moral responsibility, it reduces their moral freedom as well.

The care of young children is another case in point. Social science research consistently shows — and most Americans agree — that children are best cared for by their own mothers at home, and most mothers of young children do not want to work full-time. Sadly, many mothers feel forced into the workplace by America's punitive tax code. Bizarrely, this fuels calls for publicly supported day care centers, which would increase the need for taxes, forcing even more mothers into the workplace. (Ironically, however, financial gains realized by some mothers taking employment are mitigated by the expenses of working, such as transportation, food and clothing, and taxes.)

By preventing the family from meeting its own needs in this way, the tax code disrupts family bonding. Clearly, if a mother who would rather stay at home is forced by financial pressures to work outside the home or a father has to hold down two jobs, the time that a family has to share together is diminished. This can interfere with the development of family intimacy, reduce opportunities for teaching and playing, and prevent problems from being noted early on. Such damage to the fiber of the family reaches its sad conclusion when parents decide for financial reasons to limit the number of children that they have.

Other examples abound. Another moral responsibility is to care for one's parents and grandparents if they are no longer able to care for themselves. Again, punitive taxes and reduced economic growth make it difficult to meet this responsibility. The Social Security system and its taxes provide artificial moral cover for neglecting this responsibility. By imposing on every worker a specific tax dedicated to the provision of the elderly, government becomes a middleman, stepping between the generations and making it easy to rationalize the neglect of one's parents.

As taxation reduces savings, the ability to buy houses, meet unexpected medical bills, or provide for future security is infringed. Church and charitable giving are also squeezed out by anti-productive economic policies, and churches and charities even change in order to chase government funding.

While it limits families' freedom in ways like these, the progressive tax code also seeks deliberately to steer them into specific choices. Because progressive taxation discourages disciplined economic behavior such as saving, a number of counter-incentives have been incorporated into the tax code over the years in order to mitigate some of these perverse incentives. Examples include the mortgage interest deduction and the savings shelters like individual retirement accounts and education savings accounts. Bizarrely, many of these counter-incentives contain their own perverse incentives.

The mortgage interest deduction, for example, encourages debt. In attempting to guide people into productive economic behavior—home ownership—the tax code lures them into destructive behavior—assuming debt. The resulting rise in home prices has foreclosed for nearly all families the option of buying a home without assuming debt. And the temptation into debt surpasses merely debt for a house, as many taxpayers take out home-equity loans to purchase consumer goods in order to take the tax deduction.

The savings shelters, like IRAs, can also lead people into debt. As former Deputy Assistant Secretary of the Treasury Bruce Bartlett explains:

[T]he growth of debt is not evidence of some shortcoming by U.S. businesses and households, but the result of tax laws that give them little choice in the matter.

For individuals, debt growth results from the fact that the federal government only allows them to save in before-tax dollars in special accounts, like IRA's and 401(k)'s, that have severe withdrawal penalties. For most workers, the vast bulk of their financial assets are in such accounts. And for those with stock options, the capital gains tax will take at least 20 percent of their profits. Consequently, individual investors are virtually prohibited from selling assets to get cash for things they need and are forced to borrow instead.[15]

Again, the tax code is used to steer people into saving, but the penalties attached to these shelters coerce them into debt when they meet either hardship or opportunity.

Retirement shelters also strengthen the tax code's discouragement of work. Tax policy allows several different venues for tax-advantageous savings, but only if such savings are for retirement. Thus, the state forces people to save for a particular lifestyle or practice poor stewardship, and this coercion comes with moral consequences. By enshrining this lifestyle through tax policy, the state teaches people that they are entitled to live years without work.

By setting up tax preferences like these, the state lures its citizens into specific moral choices. Thus it intervenes in the individual's or family's own moral decision-making process and accustoms them to seek moral guidance from the government. Making virtuous choices becomes easier with practice, and governmental behavior-steering interrupts this practice.

Within the scope of appropriate behavior, there are many varied choices that one can make, and the best decision is often driven by personal or family circumstances, making it inappropriate and even foolhardy for the state to try to place its imprimatur on one decision over another. For instance, is it better to purchase a larger house or a second car? Should one prepare for the future by saving money or by returning to school? There are no universal moral absolutes regarding these questions. When government intervenes in these decisions by sanctioning some behaviors over others through tax preferences, it has again reached beyond its proper function as a minister of justice. Allowing it to do so gives it too much power, permitting it an unwarranted measure of control over citizens' lives and, by altering the costs and benefits of differing decisions, steering them into choices that they might not otherwise make.

The complexity that results from the tax code's myriad forays into social engineering creates a further intrusion in daily life. Time, money, energy, and other resources are wasted on mundane, tax-related record-keeping, planning, and calculating and re-calculating. For many families, especially those in the middle class who cannot afford professionals to shoulder the paperwork burden that their government has imposed upon them, tax-related activities consume already scarce resources, and elbow out more precious pursuits, like spending time together, reading and learning, and enjoying the arts.

As it edges out the ordinary, progressive taxation also kneecaps the extraordinary. By blunting the rewards of creativity, ingenuity, and excellence, the tax code sanctions unimaginativeness and mediocrity. Society loses the artistic accomplishments that feed the soul as well when punitive tax rates discourage creativity. As Laura Ingalls Wilder, author of the much-loved *Little House* books explained, "The more I wrote the bigger my income tax got, so I stopped."[16]

Government's presumptuous claim over private wealth is especially offensive in view of its failure to assume any of the risks or make any of the sacrifices necessary to build wealth. It becomes even more offensive in view of the positive harm that it does this pursuit through its interventionist and often irrational regulations. The government adds insult to injury when it presumes to benefit itself from the very success that it has consistently undermined. Through progressive taxation, government seizes the fruits of its citizens' hard work. It reduces citizens to chattel of the government. It exposes the lie of any claim that the citizen must pay taxes in exchange for the governmental services that he uses, for the intent of progressive taxation is to make some pay others' way through the administration of an increasingly powerful and bloated bureaucracy. Citizens' lives are reduced to uncompensated servitude to the state.

Progressive taxation assaults human dignity. Giving in to vice is a violation of human worth. It infantilizes people by rewarding those who would run to the government to impose an unnatural economic egalitarianism, rather than work hard, make wise choices, and reap the rewards of higher economic wealth and stronger character. It teaches people to believe that they can't make it without a government handicap. Perversely, this rationale only makes sense if those who have achieved economic wealth truly are superior, for otherwise there would be no need to temper their success in the name of some sort of outcome-based economics.

By fueling resentment in this way, progressive taxation undermines a nation's pursuit of the common good. It pits people against one another, encouraging citizens to view each other with the eyes of suspicion and judgment, looking to see whether someone else has more, always feeling aggrieved by the success of others. Instead of a unifying quest for the common good, policy-making becomes an adversarial competition, where special-interest groups propagate the mistaken notion that somebody must always win, and somebody must always lose.

Progressive taxation promotes moral disorder. Its perverse incentives encourage the behavior that damages society. The resulting chaos leads to unrealistic expectations of civil government to restore the order that its policies have overturned. When it tries to do so by imposing further unwise law — typically intended only to quell consequences, rather than to correct causes — it exacerbates existing problems and creates others, all the while expanding itself, increasing the dependency of its citizenry, and weakening other institutions, such as the family.

Progressive taxation elevates government above morality. It transforms the government from protector to social engineer, empowering it to forge a new kind of moral order. At the same time, it diminishes government's proper, noble role as enforcer of justice.

America's experience with progressive taxation teaches some edifying moral lessons. Ultimately, it teaches that natural order and justice prevail. Greed — individual and governmental — resentment, redistribution, and government expansionism backfire.

While the economic and moral damage done to the promise of America by progressive taxation could be disheartening, a deeper look leads to encouragement. There is a way out of America's economic and moral mess. It is to apply the lessons learned from the last century's disastrous experiment with progressive taxation and remake the tax structure into one that relies on accumulated wisdom, affirms natural justice, and fosters a climate where morality can flourish.

Section IV

TEN

Where Taxpayers' Money Goes: The Answer Nobody Knows

The rapid expansion of Americans' tax burden did not happen in a vacuum. It fueled and was fueled by a massive growth in federal spending made possible by increasing expectations of the state and decreasing expectations of other institutions. A rising tax burden both reflects and reinforces shifting expectations of government, family, church, and self, and these must be addressed directly before significant tax relief will be feasible. This section explains that America not only can afford to cut taxes but that, because of the damage done to families by expansive and often inappropriate government programming, she cannot afford not to. The section opens by illustrating the problems with current spending policy. It next traces the history of federal spending, providing insight into how the United States has arrived at this point. Finally, it discusses the moral implications of redistributionary spending programs.

Not surprisingly, higher tax revenues lead to higher spending. Analysis has shown that every one dollar increase in revenue leads to $1.59 in increased spending.[1] In other words, not only does raising tax revenues increase spending, but it even increases spending beyond the additional amounts collected. Once instituted, spending programs are difficult to repeal and budget hikes are difficult to reverse, solidifying the demand for higher and higher taxes and allowing the opponents of fiscal restraint to block tax cuts with the specious argument that the country cannot afford them. The ability of government to tax unlimited amounts leads to ever-increasing spending levels that are politically difficult to reduce.

The federal budget comprises two categories: mandatory spending and discretionary spending. Mandatory spending is primarily "entitlement" spending, i.e., the various welfare programs. This spending is considered mandatory because its levels are pre-set by law; anyone who is eligible is guaranteed a package of benefits, which the government must provide. Mandatory spending accounted for 58 percent of the federal budget in 2007; in 1965, that figure was 29 percent.[2] This represents an increase of $9,546 per household.[3]

The biggest use of discretionary money is defense. Other major sources of discretionary spending are education, training, employment, social services, and transportation. This type of spending is considered discretionary because there are no pre-set spending levels.

While the terms *mandatory* and *discretionary* are explained above according to conventional usage, such usage is not entirely accurate. On one hand, defending the nation is hardly a matter of discretion; it is a fundamental function of government. Ever-escalating welfare programming, on the other hand, is not a mandatory government service; in fact, it is not even Constitutionally legitimate, as will be explained later.

This high level of so-termed mandatory spending is a recent phenomenon. This means that entitlement spending claims an ever-growing portion of our tax money, while defense, any national government's first function, is marginalized. Because entitlement spending increases are mandatory, every year its portion of the budget grows and Congress loses more control of federal spending.

Meanwhile, bloated federal departments don't even keep track of how much tax money they're spending on what. Government's irresponsibility with the money it takes is so enormous that it didn't even audit itself as a whole until 1998. When it did, the result raised more questions than answers.

The executive branch prepared the first "Consolidated Financial Statements of the United States Government" for the budget year ending on September 30, 1997. Then, the General Accounting Office (GAO) reviewed the findings, much as outside auditors review the financial records of private companies. The GAO gave passing grades to only seven of 24 major government agencies that it reviewed. Serious deficiencies appeared in most of the government's biggest agencies, including the departments of Defense, Treasury, Transportation, Commerce, Labor, and Justice.[4] The GAO found, "[S]ignificant financial systems weaknesses, problems with fundamental record keeping, incomplete documentation, and weak internal controls . . . prevent the government from accurately reporting a large portion of its assets, liabilities, and costs."[5]

In order to balance the government's books, the GAO had to enter $12 billion in "unreconciled transactions"; this was the net difference in more than $100 billion worth of such positive and negative "unreconciled transactions." GAO found that the government could not account for "billions of dollars of property, equipment, and supplies," "accurately report major portions of the net costs of government operations," or calculate the loans it had made or guaranteed. Among the results of such ineptitude were the findings that HUD was making $900 million annually in overpayments on rent subsidies, while the Health Care Financing Administration made $23 billion in overpayments on Medicare.[6]

The GAO admitted, "Because of the government's serious systems, record-keeping, documentation, and control deficiencies, amounts reported in the consolidated financial statements and related notes do not provide a reliable source of information for decision-making by the government or the public."[7]

Senator Fred Thompson of Tennessee was more direct: "We are spending almost $2 trillion a year and managing a $850 million loan portfolio based on erroneous or non-existent information. It means basically that we don't know what the government's assets are[;] we don't know what the government's liabilities are[;] we don't know what it costs to run government."[8]

House Majority Leader Dick Armey pointed out, "If any small-business owners followed the business practices of the U.S. government, they'd quickly find themselves in jail."[9]

Vice President Al Gore was more optimistic. "The financial statement provides a roadmap to help us solve these . . . problems," he said.[10]

Speaking on condition of anonymity, a senior Clinton administration official admitted, "This is an old closet that we haven't cleaned out in 200 years."[11]

Just taking a peek behind the closet door reveals an administrative eyesore. Today's federal budget is rife with waste. According to The Heritage Foundation:

Washington makes at least $55 billion in annual program overpayments. The government's own auditors admit that 22 percent of all federal programs fail to show any positive effect on the populations they serve. Many programs are also redundant: The federal government runs 342 economic development programs, 130 programs serving the disabled, and 130 programs serving at-risk youth.[12]

The federal government also provides direct grants to states. In other words, the federal level taxes citizens and then gives the money to the states where they live. In FY 2007, the federal government spent $443.84 billion in state and local aid.[13] Much of this money is considered "pork barrel" spending, which Webster's dictionary defines as "a government appropriation . . . that provides funds for local improvements designed to ingratiate legislators with their constituents."[14]

H.L. Mencken was more blunt, charging that the American government is "a broker in pillage, and every election is a sort of advance auction sale of stolen goods."[15] For example, in fiscal year 1999,[16] the federal government sent $750,000 to Arkansas for grasshopper research, $500,000 to Starkville, Mississippi, for manure handling and disposal, and $5,136,000 to Oregon, Missouri, North Carolina, Minnesota, Maine, Michigan, Idaho, and Tennessee for wood utilization research. Refugee and entrant assistance to such non-border states as Colorado, Missouri, and Iowa totaled $12,057,000.[17] New York netted $60,393,000 for Housing Opportunities for Persons with AIDS (HOWPA); this is in addition to $98,477,000 for Housing for Special Populations. Wyoming merited $21,725,000 for Abandoned Mine Land Reclamation."[18]

While every tax cut proposal yields cries of insistence that government needs the money, government actions belie this claim. When the Mashantucket Pequot Housing Authority in Ledyard, Connecticut, tried to return $1.5 million in unused tax money to the Department of Housing and Urban Development, federal officials told the Authority to spend it on unneeded housing rather than send it back. The result was the subsidized construction of $428,000 homes for "over-income tribal members."[19]

ELEVEN

Gradual and Silent Encroachments

The course of the two centuries when America's financial closet went un-cleaned provides insight for how we reached this point. The Constitution restricts what the federal government may spend money on by specifically enumerating its powers:

> The Congress shall have Power To lay and collect Taxes, Duties, Imposts and Excises, to pay the Debts and provide for the common Defence and general Welfare of the United States; but all Duties, Imposts and Excises shall be uniform throughout the United States;
>
> To borrow Money on the credit of the United States;
>
> To regulate Commerce with foreign Nations, and among the several States, and with the Indian Tribes;
>
> To establish an uniform Rule of Naturalization, and uniform Laws on the subject of Bankruptcies throughout the United States;
>
> To coin Money, regulate the Value thereof, and of foreign Coin, and fix the Standard of Weights and Measures;
>
> To provide for the Punishment of counterfeiting the Securities and current Coin of the United States;
>
> To establish Post Offices and post Roads;
>
> To promote the Progress of Science and useful Arts, by securing for limited Times to Authors and Inventors the exclusive Right to their respective Writings and Discoveries;
>
> To constitute Tribunals inferior to the supreme Court;
>
> To define and punish Piracies and Felonies committed on the high Seas, and Offences against the Law of Nations;

To declare War, grant Letters of Marque and Reprisal, and make Rules concerning Captures on Land and Water;

To raise and support Armies, but no Appropriation of Money to that Use shall be for a longer Term than two Years;

To provide and maintain a Navy;

To make Rules for the Government and Regulation of the land and naval Forces;

To provide for calling forth the Militia to execute the Laws of the Union, suppress Insurrections and repel Invasions;

To provide for organizing, arming, and disciplining, the Militia, and for governing such Part of them as may be employed in the Service of the United States, reserving to the States respectively, the Appointment of the Officers, and the Authority of training the Militia according to the discipline prescribed by Congress;

To exercise exclusive Legislation in all Cases whatsoever, over such District (not exceeding ten Miles square) as may, by Cession of particular States, and the Acceptance of Congress, become the Seat of the Government of the United States, and to exercise like Authority over all Places purchased by the Consent of the Legislature of the State in which the Same shall be, for the Erection of Forts, Magazines, Arsenals, Dock-Yards, and other needful Buildings; And

To make all Laws which shall be necessary and proper for carrying into Execution the foregoing Powers, and all other Powers vested by this Constitution in the Government of the United States, or in any Department or Officer thereof.[1]

As James Madison, known as the Father of the Constitution, explained, the specific powers granted the government in order that it might "provide for the common Defence and general Welfare of the United States" are those that are listed immediately following these two broad objectives and that serve to qualify them.[2] Thomas Jefferson concurred: "Congress has not unlimited powers to provide for the general welfare, but only those specifically enumerated."[3]

For roughly 100 years, Constitutional restrictions were followed fairly tightly, though they almost immediately faced challenge. As early as 1794, Madison wrote disapprovingly of a $15,000 appropriation for

poverty relief. However, an intellectual foundation had been laid by Progressivism and cemented in practice by these early interventions; it would come to support a superstructure during the next century.

World War I was the major catalyst for government growth in the twentieth century. Federal spending was $713 million in 1916. It rose to nearly $19 billion in 1919 and never again fell below $2.9 billion.[17]

During the Great War, the federal government took over the ocean shipping, railroad, telephone, and telegraph industries, commandeered hundreds of manufacturing plants, began several of its own enormous corporations, ranging from ship-building to wheat trading, lent large amounts of money to businesses, regulated the private issuance of securities, established official priorities for the use of transportation facilities, food, fuel, and many raw materials, fixed the prices of dozens of commodities, intervened in the bargaining process over wages, and drafted millions of men, according to economic historian Robert Higgs.[18] National emergency became the touted justification for virtually every intrusion of federal power into the economy.

After the war's end, Warren G. Harding campaigned for the presidency on a promised return to "normalcy," but the government of the 1920s maintained higher levels of spending and taxes than those of before World War I.[19] By the end of the decade, America entered the Great Depression.

In 1928 the nation elected a president whose contradictory statements and actions regarding the proper role of government confound historians to this day. "You cannot extend the mastery of government over the daily life of a people," Herbert Hoover warned, "without somewhere making it master of people's souls and thoughts."[20] On the other hand, even before his election as president, Hoover's statements betrayed a strong desire to expand government to protect people from the vicissitudes of daily life. For example, he declared, "We in America today are nearer to the final triumph over poverty than ever before in the history of any land. The poorhouse is vanishing from among us. We have not yet reached the goal, but . . . we shall soon with the help of God be in sight of the day when poverty will be banished from this nation."[21]

The foundation of government expansion was barely dry when federal interventionism (particularly erratic monetary policy, high tariffs and income taxes, and coercive controls on production, consumption, and employment[22]) exploded into the Great Depression and led ultimately to the social damage wrought by the creation of the welfare state. In the face of this severe economic upset, moral principle fared poorly. The temptations of greed were too great to resist, and the voices of the defenders of the Constitution were drowned out by those who sought to use the power of government to solve the economic crisis.

These interventionists were unabashed in their Constitutional relativism. "I have no patience whatever with any individual who tries to hide behind the Constitution, when it comes to providing foodstuffs for our citizens," argued New York Representative Hamilton Fish in support of a 1931 hunger relief bill.[23]

"I am going to give the Constitution," said James O'Conner, a congressman from Louisiana in that same year, "the flexibility — as will enable me to vote for any measure I deem of value to the flesh and blood of my day."[24]

Seeing the political trends, even those whose hearts were not with the expansionists folded. As an Oklahoma congressman confessed, "I do not believe in this pie business, but if we are making a great big pie here — then I want to cut it into enough pieces so that Oklahoma will have its piece."[25]

For his part, Hoover greatly increased federal spending, creating a budget deficit of $2.2 billion in 1931, $1 billion of which represented transfer payments.[26] Hoover's 1929 Agricultural Marketing Act gave farmers $500 million, increased by another $100 million in 1930. In 1931 he reincarnated the War Finance Corporation as the Reconstruction Finance Corporation (RFC) as part of a nine-point program of federal intervention.[27]

Throughout the Great Depression, Hoover reiterated his belief that government must employ as many workers as possible in order to quell unemployment. In pursuit of this questionable objective, more major public works projects were started in Hoover's four years as president than in the previous thirty.[28]

In July 1932 the RFC's capital was almost doubled to $3.8 billion, and the new Emergency Relief and Construction Act gave $2.3 billion in credit and $1.6 billion in cash in that year alone.[29]

Owing to all this, the 1932 Revenue Act brought the largest peacetime tax increase in U.S. history; the top rate skyrocketed to 63 percent.[30]

Hoover applied military metaphor to economic emergency: "The battle to set our economic machine in motion in this emergency takes new forms and requires new tactics from time to time. We used such emergency powers to win the war; we can use them to fight the Depression," he said in May 1932.[31]

Uses of these "emergency powers" could be somewhat ludicrous. By 1932, the Department of Agriculture,[32] required an appropriation of $247,283,130 to provide: Cattle tuberculosis service ($6,505,800), Fungus investigations ($59,960), Blister rust investigation ($18,050), Study of worms ($78,220), Phony peach eradication ($85,000), Color investigations ($93,460), Plant dust explosions ($36,500), Bee culture ($73,920), Rabbit experiment station ($12,640), Food habits of birds study ($107,660), Pink boll worm control ($497,000), and more.

The growing paternalism reached absurd proportions. Housed under the Department of Agriculture, the Bureau of Home Economics designed trousers "for the very small child who is just learning to dress himself." Advertising these tax-paid pants in No. 52 of more than 160 pamphlets it issued, the Bureau explained: "The trousers worn by the little boy in the picture can be buttoned to an underwaist, as shown, with a matching or contrasting loose blouse over it. Or, when the weather becomes warm and the days invitingly sunshiny, the underwaist may be replaced by an open mesh sunsuit top of cable net."[33]

While federal paternalism was on the increase, paternal authority in the family was in decline. Social workers found again and again that unemployment weakened the father's authority in the family. One study concluded that one-fifth of its sample of 59 families exhibited a breakdown in the father's authority, particularly in the eyes of his wife. One woman said, "When your husband cannot provide for the family and makes you worry so, you lose your love for him." In another family whose father was unemployed for a long time, his oldest son assumed the paternal role. Said the father himself, "He tries to settle any little brother-and-sister fights and even encourages me and my wife." Another of the family's sons who was also working described his relationship with his parents: "I remind them . . . who makes the money. They don't say much. They just take it[;] that's all. I'm not the one on relief."[34]

Hoover's waffling between pro-freedom rhetoric and interventionist action satisfied virtually no one. The economic insecurity of the Great

Depression led to popular sentiment in favor of a strong political leader. In February 1933, *Barron's* claimed, "[A] mild species of dictatorship will help us over the roughest spots in the road ahead."[35] Perhaps unwittingly revealing the link between progressivism and fascism, *The Nation* published an article titled, "Wanted: A Mussolini."[36] Proposals to revive the authoritarianism of World War I proliferated.[37]

In 1932 the country elected Franklin Delano Roosevelt as president. In his 1933 inaugural address Roosevelt unhesitatingly grabbed for the power that the country was offering. Just as Hoover likened the country's economic woes to war, he claimed the existence of a state of emergency and called for unprecedented government power to solve it:

> [W]e must move as a trained and loyal army willing to sacrifice for the good of a common discipline. . . . [T]he larger purposes will bind upon us all as a sacred obligation with a unity of duty hitherto evoked only in time of armed strife. . . . I assume unhesitatingly the leadership of this great army of our people. . . . [I]n the event that the Congress shall fail to [act] . . . and in the event that the national emergency is still critical . . . I shall ask the Congress for . . . broad executive power to wage a war against the emergency as great as the power that would be given me if we were in fact invaded by a foreign foe.[38]

According to Senator James Byrnes, the situation warranted that "principles as well as policies . . . be temporarily subordinated to the necessity of some experimentation in order to preserve the government itself."[39]

The New Deal was the amalgamation of unprecedented interventionist monetary, fiscal, and regulatory federal policies during the 1930s. The New Deal inaugurated federal spending programs explicitly designed to redistribute wealth. Social Security and unemployment assistance first began during the era, as did the system of farm price supports and other agricultural subsidies.[40]

The major relief agencies were the National Recovery Administration (NRA), the Federal Emergency Relief Administration (FERA), the Civil Works Administration (CWA), the Civilian Conservation Corps (CCC), the Works Progress Administration (WPA), and the Social Security Board (SSB). The FERA, CWA, CCC, and WPA programs combined elements of public works with public relief through the administration of large work relief programs.[41] New Deal public works jobs included raking leaves, mowing grass, and shooing pigeons from the eaves of public buildings.[42]

In addition, the New Deal encompassed: efforts to reflate the economy by means of Department of Treasury purchases of silver and gold and by government cartelization schemes, including the Agricultural Adjustment Administration (AAA), increases in regulation, and, of course, high tax-and-spend fiscal policy that spawned sky-rocketing deficits.[43]

Many New Deal programs trace their roots back to World War I. The Food and Fuel Administrations became models for New Deal agencies.[44] The Tennessee Valley Authority originated with a dam originally launched by the Defense Act of 1916.[45] World War I housing agencies were reborn in the New Deal.[46] Members of the War Industries Board helped create the NRA.[47]

By 1934, twenty million Americans were on the dole.[48] Federal spending grew by 136 percent from 1932 to 1940.[49] During 1933 to 1939, the federal government spent $27,435,135,624 on New Deal programming, representing 55 percent of total federal spending.[50]

After Hoover imposed a set of policies that significantly enlarged the function and role of the federal government in the national economy, Roosevelt's programs fundamentally reshaped American government itself: They shifted the bulk of government spending from the local level to the federal, concentrated power in the executive branch, imposed enormous bureaucratic control of private business, and began direct federal financial support of certain citizens.

Well-to-do progressive newspaper editor William Allen White was ecstatic. Roosevelt was, he wrote:

> aiming at something of the same target at which both the fascists and the communists are shooting[,] that is to say, the socialization of capital, the regimentation of industry and agriculture, and finally, a more equitable distribution of wealth, a guarantee of a minimum standard of living for all who have worked honestly. . . . Probably America can do this strange thing—establish a new revolution of free men with their dollars in shackles.

Recounting the specific victories in this "revolution," White glowed:

> We have clamored for higher income taxes, for devastating inheritance taxes, for workmen's compensation, unemployment insurance, old-age pension. . . . It is plain as a barn door that we are getting our revolution through the administrative arm of the government, without legislation. . . . These are great days—if not happy ones.[51]

In the beginning, the courts did not fully support the legislative and executive branches' extra-Constitutional reach. Early programs were struck down. By the end of 1936, federal judges had issued approximately 1,600 injunctions to restrain federal officials from carrying out acts of Congress.[52]

As the Great Depression and Roosevelt's presidency wore on, defense of the Constitution wore out. On the one hand, in United States v. Butler (1936), the Supreme Court ruled against the agricultural part of the first New Deal on the grounds that a tax levied on processors to support farmers was "the expropriation of money from one group for the benefit of another."[53] In other words, such fiscal redistribution was still recognized as unconstitutional.

On the other hand, the Court asserted in the same case, "The power of Congress to authorize appropriations of public money for public purposes is not limited by the grants of legislative power found in the Constitution."[54]

Nothing could be more contrary to the intentions of the Founders. Madison himself had torpedoed the anti-federalists making this claim as entirely disingenuous:

> It has been urged and echoed, that the power "to lay and collect taxes, duties, imposts, and excises, to pay the debts, and provide for the common defense and general welfare of the United States," amounts to an unlimited commission to exercise every power which may be alleged to be necessary for the common defense or general welfare. No stronger proof could be given of the duress under which these writers labor for objections, than their stooping to such a misconstruction. Had no other enumeration or definition of the powers of the Congress be found in the Constitution, than the general expressions just cited,

the authors of the objection might have had some color for it; though it would have been difficult to find a reason for so awkward a form of describing an authority to legislate in all possible cases. . . . [W]hat color can the objection have, when a specification of the objects alluded to by these general terms immediately follows, and is not even separated by a longer pause than a semicolon? If the different parts of the same instrument ought to be so expounded, as to give meaning to every part which will bear it, shall one part of the same sentence be excluded altogether from a share in the meaning . . . shall the more doubtful and indefinite terms be retained in their full extent, and the clear and precise expressions be denied any signification whatsoever? For what purpose could the enumeration of particular powers be inserted, if these and all others were meant to be included in the preceding general power? Nothing is more natural nor common than first to use a general phrase, and then to explain and qualify it by a recital of particulars. . . . [T]he idea of an enumeration of particulars which neither explain nor qualify the general meaning, and can have no other effect than to confound and mislead, is an absurdity, which, as we are reduced to the dilemma of charging either on the authors of the objection or on the authors of the Constitution, we must take the liberty of supposing, had not its origin with the latter.[55]

Elsewhere in *The Federalist*, he wrote:

The powers delegated by the proposed Constitution to the federal government are few and defined. . . . The[y] . . . will be exercised principally on external objects, as war, peace, negotiation, and foreign commerce; with which last the power of taxation will, for the most part, be connected. . . . The operations of the federal government will be most extensive and important in times of war and danger . . .[56]

Many New Deal programs last to this day. Some are absurd anachronisms. Others are taken for granted, such as Unemployment Compensation and Workers' Compensation. Aid to Families with Dependent Children (AFDC) has been retooled into Temporary Assistance to Needy Families (TANF), which limits benefit eligibility to five years, requires some recipients to work thirty hours per week (though educational pursuits are considered work for some of these hours), and gives states more latitude in finding solutions to welfare dependency. Originally, these programs were intended to serve populations in need for reasons beyond their control. AFDC was intended to care for widows with small children. As Charles Murray explains, "Nothing in the New Deal provided help just because a person was poor or hampered by social disadvantages."[57]

No other social welfare program has approached the profound consequences of the Social Security system. Social Security has three main components. The largest and best known is the old age insurance component that pays benefits after retirement. Survivors insurance pays benefits to any dependent children of a deceased wage earner. Finally, disability insurance pays benefits to disabled workers who have paid into the system.

Promoted as an "insurance" program into which everybody pays and from which everybody takes, Social Security's history has shown the program to be at best another transfer program and at worst a Ponzi scheme.

According to Martha Derthick of the Brookings Institution, "In the mythic construction began in 1935 and elaborated thereafter on the basis of the payroll tax, Social Security was a vast enterprise of self-help in which government participation was almost incidental."[58]

Former Social Security Commissioner Stanford Ross criticized the founders of the social security for generating public support by advancing the fictitious belief that a worker "pays for" benefits with "contributions" rather than taxes, and has an "earned right" to particular benefits. Ross advised Americans to reject the "myth" that Social Security is a pension plan and accept it as a tax on workers to provide for the "vulnerable in our society."[59]

Senator Patrick Moynihan went further, calling Social Security taxes "outright thievery" from young working people.[60]

Social Security has been a powerful engine of government growth. First, it now represents more than one-fifth of the entire federal budget. Second, it has enabled creative accounting techniques that have hidden spending. Throughout history, the Social Security system has historically taken in more in taxes than it has paid out. (Analysts expect that this might change as early as 2009, when the system will begin to pay out more than it brings in, if fundamental changes are not made.) These Social Security surpluses have been lent to the rest of the federal government to fund other programs. In exchange, the government has written the Social Security system IOUs; these IOUs comprise the so-called Social Security Trust Fund. These Social Security loans to the rest of the government have permitted the government to spend beyond its means.

As New Deal schemes grew, the Depression continued, until Roosevelt was aided by ironic allies: Japanese bombers. What little the Depression — and the misapplication of war metaphors to it — could not accomplish in government growth, real war could. Constitutional scholar Edward Corwin writes that Court sanction during World War II solidified:

(1) the attribution to Congress of a legislative power of indefinite scope;
(2) the attribution to the President of the power and duty to stimulate constantly the positive exercise of this indefinite power for enlarged social objectives;
(3) the right of Congress to delegate its powers *ad libitum* to the President for the achievement of such enlarged social objectives . . .;
(4) the attribution to the President of a broad prerogative in the meeting of "emergencies" defined by himself and in the creation of executive agencies to assist him;
(5) a progressively expanding replacement of the judicial process by the administrative process in the enforcement of the law — sometimes even of constitutional law.[61]

American socialist Michael Harrington praised the impact of war in promoting government growth: "During World War II, there was probably more of an increase in social justice than at any [other] time in American history. Wage and price controls were used to try to cut the differentials between the social classes. . . . There was also a powerful moral incentive to spur workers on: patriotism."[62]

At the end of World War II, defense spending dropped dramatically, and taxes were lowered slightly. By 1948 the United States had its biggest surplus in modern times — almost $12 billion or more than 4 percent of gross domestic product. A year later, federal spending had increased by more than 30 percent, and the surplus was gone. More than 60 percent of this increase went to national security and foreign policy demands created by the Cold War and the Marshall Plan.[63]

In 1956, the United States again enjoyed a surplus, only to squander it by 1958. While tax revenues rose by a significant 7.2 percent, more than twice the rate of inflation, spending grew rapidly. There were large increases in foreign aid, funds for school buildings, and the interstate highway system, while expenditures for "social security" and "income security" alone rose a whopping 18 percent.[64]

The next significant episode of federal expansionism would be the Great Society. Within three years of assuming the Presidency in 1963, Lyndon Johnson had requested 200 major pieces of legislation; Congress approved 181 of them. Roosevelt had peddled the drug of government give-aways primarily in the poor neighborhoods; Johnson set up shop in middle-class cul-de-sacs, and most Americans, willingly or unwillingly, wittingly or unwittingly, are forced to shoot up. Johnson's sweeping proposals sought to address almost every issue of concern to Americans: civil rights, poverty, education, health, housing, pollution, the arts, cities, occupational safety, consumer protection, and mass transit, to name only the most prominent. "LBJ adopted programs, his aide Joseph Califano later noted, 'the way a child eats rich chocolate-chip cookies,'" reports Johnson biographer John Andrew.[65]

Congress easily passed Johnson's Economic Opportunity Bill of 1964, which created a new federal agency, the Office of Economic Opportunity (OEO), and ten programs: the Neighborhood Youth Corps; the Work Experience Project, the Adult Basic Education Program (ABE), the Rural Loan Program, the College Work Study Program, the Job Corps; Volunteers in Service to America (VISTA), the Community Action Program, and the Migrant Assistance Program (MAP). Congress appropriated $800 million for the first year of this War on Poverty.[66]

The 1964 annual report of the Council of Economic Advisers openly explained the dangers of the transfer society: "Conquest of poverty is well within our power. The majority of the nation could simply tax themselves enough to provide the necessary income supplements to their less fortunate citizens. . . . [T]his 'solution' would leave untouched most of the roots of poverty. Americans want to *earn* the American standard by their own efforts and contributions."[67] Regrettably, the warning was not heeded, and the consequences have been tragic.

The War on Poverty was doomed to failure from the beginning. As the National Association of Manufacturers (NAM) warned, if "the program were to be expanded so as to reach all the cases it is intended to help . . . it would have to be many times larger. The cost would then reach a point where it would seriously impede the growth of the private economy. Thus you seem to have a choice between a program which is so small as to be ineffective, and one so large as to be damaging."[68]

According to John Andrew,

> The Economic Opportunity Act sought to give Americans a chance to escape poverty and prepare young people for education and work. . . . The act suffered from hasty preparation, an absorption with racial and urban problems, and a failure to confront the underlying causes of poverty. Consequently its proposals were fragmented. Each section of the act sought a separate remedy to the problem of poverty[;] thus no coordinated program emerged.[69]

Despite its failures, Congress in 1965 nearly doubled its authorization for OEO programs to $1.5 billion.[70] Between 1965 and 1972, Congress spent $15 billion on the War on Poverty.[71] Total federal expenditures from 1965 to 1973 more than doubled from $118 billion to $260 billion.[72]

Medicare and Medicaid were created in 1965. Immediately, the price of health care rose. Federal expenditures on health services and facilities rose nearly ten-fold from $2.9 billion in 1959–60 to $20.6 billion in 1970–71. Institutionalized patient charges rose by one-third from 1965 to 1967, while individuals' out-of-pocket costs dropped by 15 percent.[73] Health expenditures for the poor skyrocketed from $1.6 billion in 1966 to $5.1 billion just two years later.[74]

The Social Security Amendments of 1967 increased Social Security benefits by 13 percent, to be paid for by raising both the Social Security tax rate and the wage base, continuing the transformation of Social Security from an old-age assistance program to an antipoverty program and accelerating the financial drain upon the system. In addition, Medicare was made more permissive, covering previously excluded services. Cost-cutting changes were made to Medicaid, but the federal contribution toward the cost of medical personnel working in state Medicaid programs increased from 50 to 75 percent. Finally, the legislation mandated work-training for AFDC recipients and provided for the creation of day-care centers for children whose mothers were working or in training.[75]

Launching the War on Poverty, Johnson declared, "[T]he days of the dole are numbered." Within two generations, more than $10 trillion have been spent on this war,[76] more in current dollars than was spent to win World War II.

Johnson's programming was significant as more than a spending spree. The War on Poverty defined poverty and unemployment alleviation as the responsibility of the federal government and ingrained the twentieth-century notion that government should play an active role in shaping people's lives. As Johnson biographer John Andrew notes, "Perhaps the major contribution of the War on Poverty is that it focused attention on a fundamental issue and argued that deliberate policymaking rather than casual economic growth was necessary if all citizens were to share in the promise of American life."[77]

This transformation of government's role from protector of rights to provider of services created moral confusion that helped redefine its new services as "rights." Andrew explains, "[T]he poor could seek leverage by organizing and exerting 'their political muscle.' They did so in 1967 with the formation of the National Welfare Rights Organization (NWRO). The NWRO had an impact. By the early 1970s the number of lawyers focusing on poverty issues had risen by 650 percent, and they appealed 164 cases to the Supreme Court. Welfare was now seen as less of a stigma and more of a 'right.'"[78]

At the same time, education also came to be perceived as a right. Johnson steered at least sixty education laws through Congress.[79] Johnson signed the Elementary and Secondary Education Act (ESEA) on April 11, 1965. It provided for aid to poor children in slums and rural areas, created a five-year program for school libraries to buy textbooks and other instructional materials, established a five-year program of grants to the states to create supplemental educational centers and services, provided for educational research and strengthened state departments of education. Debate over the bill recalled earlier controversies regarding proper limits to federal intervention.

Representative John Anderson explained: "This is a very fundamental debate between those who think education is simply not a federal function and those who do[,] between those who think it is something that constitutionally, historically, and traditionally has been reserved to the States and those who think otherwise."[80]

Representative Charles Goodell warned that the bill's "clear intent is to radically change our historic structure of education by a dramatic shift of power to the federal level."[81]

Representative Howard Smith warned, "[W]e apparently have come to the end of the road so far as local control over our education in public facilities is concerned."[82]

Representative Clarence Brown, Jr., called the bill "one of the most dangerous measures that has come before us in my time."[83]

Johnson also introduced or expanded federal involvement in an array of private concerns, from health and housing to the arts. However, expansion of the federal role did not forge expansion of its natural capabilities. Andrew writes:

> Too often Johnson deliberately understated the continuing costs of new programs and requested only modest funding, hoping that once under way neither Congress nor the public would desert them. This led him to begin more programs than the bureaucracy, the public, or the budget could digest at one time. It also led him to overpromise, to insist that each new endeavor was not only essential but represented *the* solution to complex and perplexing problems. . . . [L]aws are not an end in themselves. As White House aide Joseph Califano admitted, "We did not recognize that government could not do it all."[84] [italics in original]

Of course, the Founders did. Government cannot provide its citizens with every good thing; it cannot protect them from every bad thing, and it cannot synthesize new rights by violating the natural ones. Whenever it tries, it creates bigger problems than those it misguidedly sought to solve. Abandoning the principles enshrined in the Constitution in order to experiment with practical changes allows the establishment of structures, policies, and programs that are contrary to the *raison d'être* of a Constitutional republic. Subordinating principle to practicality is counterproductive. Only principle endures long term. Practical concerns, by their nature, are transient. Over time, this pulls a nation further and further from its own ideological foundation, until there remains only a vague awareness that it was ever intended to serve higher ends than meeting immediate, practical concerns. This promotes an unhealthy reliance upon the state to provide what it is not charged to provide, while at the same time undermining its ability to protect the rights it is instituted to secure. Such has been the legacy of the twentieth century.

TWELVE

Bail-Out Nation

In late 2008, wealth redistribution reached new absurdity in the form of two bail-outs forced through by the Bush administration that transferred hundreds of billions of tax-payers' dollars to supposedly troubled big corporations.

First came the bank bailout, for which Congress appropriated a whopping $700 Billion. Next was the auto bailout, for which President George W. Bush siphoned more than $17 Billion from the bank bail-out after the Senate refused to pass a bill allocating additional moneys.

Industry bailouts like these are part of what's considered "corporate welfare," which Dean Stansel of the Cato Institute defines as "any government *spending* program that provides unique benefits or advantages to specific companies or industries" [italics in original].

Stansel identifies three main categories of corporate welfare. First, there are direct grants to businesses. Stansel cites as "perhaps the most egregious example of corporate welfare" the Agriculture Department's $90 million per year Market Access Program (MAP), which redistributes taxpayers' money to exporters of food and other agricultural products to offset the costs of overseas advertising.

Second, there are programs that provide research and other services for industries. For example, the Department of Energy's (DOE) Energy Supply Research and Development program works with private-sector firms to develop and improve energy technologies at an annual cost to the taxpayers of $1.9 billion.

Third, there are programs that provide subsidized loans or insurance to private companies. In one such instance, the Export-Import Bank annually spends $700 million of taxpayers' money to provide subsidized financing to foreign purchasers of U.S. goods through the use of direct loans and below-market interest rates, loan guarantees to private lenders, and subsidized export credit insurance. The average delinquency rate for such loan programs is almost three times that for commercial lenders.[1]

The 2008 bail-outs, and the way they were foisted on an unwilling public, tell much of the story of what's gone wrong with American fiscal policy-making. The so-called crises that these bail-outs were purported to quell were significantly sparked by a government-nurtured entitlement mentality. Both bail-outs were rationalized with appeals to that same sense of entitlement, and both were rushed through with the claims that the American economy would plunge into deeper recession or even depression without them. But despite the scare tactics and naked appeals to consumerism, the people didn't want these bail-outs. They rejected the moral hazard of rewarding massive malfeasance, and they rejected saddling their children and grandchildren with trillion-dollar debt.

While Secretary of the Treasury Henry Paulson outdid his predecessor Alexander Hamilton in grasping at federal power, an obviously muddled President Bush spoke nonsense about keeping the market economy moving via massive federal intervention. Corporate welfare stems from confusion regarding the role of government. Politicians and pundits frequently insist that government must keep the economy stable and strong. What they miss is that government should and can best nurture a strong economy by protecting the rights to freedom and property whose appropriate exercise creates wealth. When instead government misuses its power to rob middle-class families and small businesses in order to keep big corporations afloat, it corrodes the order in which prosperity can best flourish. And when this perversion of its proper role is expensive enough, the corrosion reaches down into generations not yet even born.

The people recognized the moral hazard of propping up failing corporations on the backs of babies yet to be born and rejected Bush's bail-outs. But the despots sneered, and took hostages in Omelas.

THIRTEEN

The Moral Hazard of Spreading the Wealth

America's Founders had recognized that the government could not do everything, and that it shouldn't try. Constitutional limits are not arbitrary, and the consequences of their abandonment are not coincidental. These limits are the product of centuries of thought on the proper role of government; they are intended to protect against encroachment and the damage that ensues when it oversteps its limits, guided by the vicissitudes of public opinion instead of transcendent ideals. When these limits are overthrown or ignored, the state seizes responsibility for which it is neither intended nor equipped. Usurping the authority of other institutions, it weakens them, and creates tremendous harm.

Foremost among these institutions is family — the bedrock of any civilized society. It is the family, not the state, that can best fill such functions as the nurture and education of children, the care of the elderly, and so on. Neither intended nor equipped to serve in this role, the state does a poor job and leaves family and society to cope with the morally disastrous results of its bungling.

Seventy years of welfare policy have devastated the family in the poor community. By paying women to have children outside wedlock, welfare has created an underclass, nearly caste-like in its inescapability, of people who don't even know anyone who's married. With its ever-increasing role in providing childcare, the government has weakened the parent-child bond and promoted the absurd idea that a paid attendant can replicate the love and nurture of a family. Tragically, because of the excessive tax burden and the usurpation of its authority, the family is left less capable of mitigating the damage caused by its own weakening.

This weakening of the family empowers government while eroding respect for the family and further increasing its dependency on the state. This influences both personal and policy decisions. Public policy that affects the family cannot be evaluated properly without respect for the family as the backbone of society. This means that initiatives that would damage the family are not treated with proper trepidation, while those that would restore its primacy are rejected.

In addition, individual choices are compromised as both men and women have less incentive to commit to their own families. When the state usurps the role of providing practical support, it makes it easier for men to abandon their families. Further, by weakening the esteem in which the family is held, the state also diminishes the allure of leadership of the family. In the same way, by eroding respect for the family, the state diminishes respect for providing care and nurture within the family. Thus women also have less incentive to meet their familial responsibilities. The consequent family breakdown leads to social breakdown in the form of various pathologies such as crime, unwed pregnancy, etc., costing society in terms of safety, morality, and money.

Further, by usurping the authority of the family, the state blurs understanding of the proper spheres and scope of authority. The institutions of family, church, and state are naturally suited to fill different roles. When one institution usurps the authority of another, it threatens our understanding of the proper limits to authority and of what we can expect and not expect from each institution. When one institution, in this case the government, attempts to meet an ever-growing number of our needs, we lose any sense that there should be limits on what it does.

In the same way, when the state usurps the role of religious institutions, it diminishes regard for them, making them appear ineffectual, and discourages people from giving of their time and resources to their work. More grievously, people are discouraged from turning to these institutions and hearing their life-changing message.

While the direct devastation that interventionist policies cause family and church has been tremendous, more insidious is what the ever-growing government has done to our national character and our understanding of right and wrong. Labeling the state's taking from one person to bestow upon another *legal plunder*, French philosopher Frederic Bastiat points out that such immoral action perverts the very purpose of government. He writes:

Each of us has a natural right—from God—to defend his person, his liberty, and his property . . .

If every person has the right to defend . . . his person, his liberty, and his property, then it follows that a group of men have the right to organize and support a common force to protect these rights constantly. Thus the principle of collective right—its reason for existing, its lawfulness—is based on individual right. . . . [T]he common force that protects this collective right cannot logically have any other purpose or any other mission than that for which it acts as a substitute. Thus, since an individual cannot lawfully use force against the person, liberty, or property of another individual, then the common force—for the same reason—cannot lawfully be used to destroy the person, liberty, or property of individuals or groups.

Such a perversion of force would be, in both cases, contrary to our premise. Force has been given to us to defend our own individual rights. Who will dare . . . say that force has been given to us to destroy the equal rights of our brothers? Since no individual acting separately can lawfully use force to destroy the rights of others, does it not logically follow that the same principle also applies to the common force that is nothing more than the organized combination of the individual forces?

The law is the organization of the natural right of lawful defense. It is the substitution of a common force for individual forces. . . . [T]his common force is to do only what the individual forces have a natural and lawful right to do: to protect persons, liberties, and properties; to maintain the right of each, and to cause *justice* to reign over us all.

[U]nfortunately, law by no means confines itself to its proper functions. . . . [W]hen it has exceeded proper functions, it has not done so merely in some inconsequential and debatable matters. The law has gone further than this; it has acted in direct opposition to its own purpose. The law has been used to destroy its own objective: It has been applied to annihilating the justice that it was supposed to maintain; to limiting and destroying rights which its real purpose was to respect. . . . It has converted plunder into a right, in order to protect plunder.[1]

Acknowledging that, for many people, what is legal is legitimate, Bastiat explains that immoral state actions cause confusion: "When law and morality contradict each other, the citizen has the cruel alternative of either losing his moral sense or losing his respect for the law."[2]

It is not difficult to argue that America has lost both. The message that someone else's rights pose absolutely no legitimate obstacle to one's desire has sunk in; this is evident in situations such as abortion and the fact that kids are killing each other over sneakers and leather jackets. Such disheartening social trends as the rudeness that is much lamented of late, the adultery that isn't, road rage, and instant intimacy are attributable to many factors, but fiscal policy that encourages disrespect for others by deluding one into thinking that he is somehow entitled to what belongs to someone else is surely one of them.

His moral compass thus thrown off by the magnet of unjust policy, the citizen is more likely to respond to its perverse incentives. Progressive taxation and redistributive spending policies encourage laziness among both those who are taxed and those who are given. Those who are taxed at increasing rates are discouraged from work because they receive diminishing fruits from their labors. Those who receive are discouraged because they receive without having to work at all. Beyond the daily laziness of simply not working, or working less, there is the more dangerous moral laziness of not taking responsibility for one's own life. Finally, there is the disincentive to marriage, as it can leave beneficiaries ineligible for so-called entitlements.

Many even come to perceive benefits provided through the auspices of the state at the forced expense of others as rights. This perception is reflected even the official term *entitlements* for many of these benefits. This flawed perception stems in part from the moral confusion resulting when government oversteps in proper limits. Taught from young ages "that to secure . . . rights governments are instituted,"[3] citizens logically if incorrectly come to believe that whatever it provides is ours by right.

However, presuming to provide for our every need, the government violates our rights. Both the coerced providers and their recipients are morally diminished. Forced to surrender the fruits of their labor to others, the providers are enslaved in the truest sense: they are forced to work for others. The dependency of the recipients is a form of slavery as well, for in dependency is loss of freedom. Thus the politics of redistribution, seeking to elevate the have-nots by robbing the haves reduces both to a symbiotic slavery; each is enslaved by the other.

Complicating matters is the fact that there is no firm delineation between the providers and the takers. The middle class especially is subject to oppressively high taxation to fuel the redistributionary state, but at the same time it is dependent on the provision of the state. The irony is that it is largely excessive taxation that renders us so dependent on government provision. Thus we live under a bizarre form of fiscal mercantilism whereby we send our tax dollars to the government and have them returned to us in the form of services over which we have no control. This occurs at the individual level, but also at the state level. Federal aid to states has turned them from the largely independently functioning entities envisioned by the Framers into mere administrative vassals of the massive federal leviathan.

A deeper irony is that the arrogant presumption that others should meet one's needs stems from a (probably unwitting) view of others as more capable. The state agrees with this bizarre and dangerous combination of moral weakness and sense of entitlement; the implicit message in providing for some at the expense of others is that some are just not capable of taking care of themselves. While laws against private theft tell thieves and would-be thieves, "We expect better of you," redistributionary policies say the opposite: "We don't expect much from you."

The sometimes hysterical rhetoric against welfare reform makes clear that this point is penetrating. In an open letter to President Clinton, Julia Star, a self-described honors student working towards two computer associates' degrees and a recipient of TANF, Food Stamps, Medicaid, and Child Care, labels the 30-hour per week work requirement for welfare recipients "extreme." Ms. Star complains about having "to spend literally every waking moment studying" to avoid having to pay back her Pell and OIG grants, her 8 AM to 4 PM Workfare hours, and the fact that her 14-year-old son "has to cook the meals, do laundry and help with his 4-year-old sister . . . among other things" while she has no time to play with her daughter.[4]

Nowhere in her two-page jeremiad does Ms. Star accept any responsibility for her situation or for improving it, nor does she show any regard for the millions of working families sacrificing better education in order to pay for hers.

At the same time, transfer policies discourage the individual from fulfilling his moral duty to care for the truly needy. When people pressure for high taxes on the most prosperous to pay for care of the poor, they are engaging in a kind of moral buck-passing, for they want the provision for the needy to come at someone else's expense. When these demands are met, the middle-class citizen can ignore his own responsibility to care for others at his own, sometimes sacrificial, expense. This actually robs him of the moral strengthening that comes from fulfilling duty. Virtue is made easier with practice; to give synthetic moral cover to those who would shirk their responsibilities is to discourage them from growing in virtue by practicing it.

Meanwhile, presuming to provide for their every need, the state renders the people susceptible to demagoguery. The first solution to any problem is increased government involvement. Many don't even think to look further, to ask whether another institution might better solve the problem or even whether it can really be solved with anybody's intervention. Even some self-proclaimed supporters of limited government are seduced by the allure of easy federal money. Politicians, far from promising to protect rights, instead send out glossy mailers promising to take care of every need, with bones tossed to every interest group, and that is increasingly the basis on which elections are decided. Citizens become infantilized. Every extension of government makes them more dependent and weakens them against its encroachments.

Further, government inefficiency exacerbates the damage that it does to the nation. Massive increases in federal funds for education have coincided with declining student scores, for example. Between 1960 and 1990, spending on elementary and secondary education jumped from $50 billion to nearly $190 billion in inflation-adjusted dollars. During the same period, per student spending more than tripled—from $1,454 to $4,622. Between 1973 and 1993, public school spending increased by 47 percent while per pupil spending increased by 62 percent. At the same time, the total number of teachers increased by only 17 percent while non-teaching positions mushroomed by 40 percent. Despite all the spending, student performance on the SATs declined from 1960 to 1990. As the ranks of ill-prepared high school graduates swelled and they entered college, U.S. university dropout rates climbed to among the highest in the industrialized world—37 percent.[5]

Further, the politics of redistribution are not confined to financial support. In many cases, the state goes beyond merely overstepping its role to actually funding outright evil. Pornographic "art" and contraception for unwed minors, for example, are made possible by our massive federal budget, diminishing the moral climate of the nation and reducing those who object to funding such outrages to moral slavery.

Many Americans recognize the failures of Big Brother. A 1996 Gallup Poll found that 50 percent of Americans believe, "[T]he federal government has become so large and powerful that it poses an immediate threat to the rights and freedoms of ordinary citizens."[6]

A 1995 national survey conducted for the federally funded Council for Excellence in Government (CEG) revealed that 72 percent of respondents agreed, "[T]he federal government creates more problems than it solves"; only 21 percent said that it solves more problems than it creates.[7] Fifty-six percent of the respondents said that government programs and policies do more to hinder than help their families "in trying to achieve the American dream"; only 31 percent responded that government does more to help than hinder.

Specifically measuring the attitudes of those who partake of government largesse, the poll found, in the words of *New Democrat* magazine, "47 percent of those whose everyday existence relies to some extent on government aid replied that this same government was a hindrance to their achieving the American dream."[8]

History has made clear that fiscal redistribution has not lived up to its promises. While many programs have been imposed under the rhetoric of serving the common good by providing support for the needy, they have, in fact, done moral damage to all involved. Redistributionary fiscal policies have subverted the Constitution, fostered family fragmentation, encouraged laziness, quenched creativity, and created a leviathan state on which nearly everybody depends. They have hurt the people they are intended to help and transformed government from servant to master. It is morally vital to curtail them.

Section V

FOURTEEN

Principles of Sound Fiscal Reform

In August 1173, workers in the small town of Pisa, Italy, began construction on a bell tower for the city's cathedral. Construction continued for two centuries, during which time the tower started to incline. After the inclination appeared in the first three floors, the builders tried to compensate by building the upper floors to lean the other way. This simply over-corrected the problem, and the tower began to incline in the opposite direction. Later, damaged columns and other parts had to be replaced on more than one occasion. Still today, work continues in the tower's sub-soil to reduce its inclination and prevent it from collapsing.

An inherently unsound structure cannot be stabilized. Like a structurally flawed building, America's tax law cannot simply be fixed. It is beyond repair and should be scrapped. If it is to be recreated in a way that will not cause unnecessary harm, it must be done according to sound principles. This chapter draws on lessons from earlier chapters and offers a set of principles to guide fiscal reform.

Any useful structure or system is designed and built according to its purpose. Ships are structured to carry passengers and cargo over seas, houses to supports families' living needs, factories to facilitate production. If the materials used to support physical structures conflict with their purposes, the structures themselves undermine their own *raisons d'être*. Weak fastenings sink ships and their cargoes; asbestos-laden insulation threatens family health; faulty wiring burns down factories and the goods they produce.

The government exists to maintain justice; taxes are imposed to supply the revenues needed to meet this purpose. An unjust tax system compromises the ability of the government it feeds to maintain justice.

Prudent tax law—which serves rather than undermines government's purpose—must be crafted according to a vision of the just society that it is intended to support in deference to the natural order that rewards virtue and punishes vice.

Any sound economic strategy ignores the clamor of resentment and rejects the partiality of imposing different rules for different people. It avoids anything to discourage the virtuous behavior that creates wealth. This means rejecting the graduated tax brackets that apply only to some, and discarding an alternative minimum tax or similar scheme that sets up an entire parallel tax system against a minority. The tax code should also be free from specific favors targeted to certain groups. These favors interfere with moral decisions by steering citizens into state-sanctioned choices. The tax code instead should honor the fact that people, not the government, are the best moral decision-makers.

Respect for privacy was one of the hallmarks of America's founding, and this respect should be reflected in today's tax code. Citizens ideally would not be required to reveal their income, sources of income, saving, spending, and investment choices, or any other private financial information.

Taxes should not be multiplicative; taxpayers should not be subject to the fiscal double-jeopardy of paying two, three, or four times on the same money. Citizens should not, for instance, have to pay income and payroll taxes on the same earnings or multiple layers of tax (i.e., corporate, individual, capital gains, and estate) on investment earnings.

The tax code should have some stability. Otherwise, it invites all the damage against which James Madison warned in Federalist 66. It should not be changed every year or two, or changed so frequently that further changes are made before the earlier ones are even implemented. The tax system should be viewed as a whole and not altered piecemeal, creating a structure that is incomprehensible, at odds with itself, and rife with unforeseen consequences.

The tax code should be altered only after careful consideration of what the effects of any changes will be. This means thinking through their logical impact on people's behavior. Marginal rate increases tend not to produce commensurate revenue increases; on the contrary, revenues increase, and increase especially from the "rich", when marginal rates are cut, as the experience of the 1920s, '60s, and '80s shows.

While it is tempting to raise taxes during wars and other national crises and purported crises, no longer are these increases automatically undone after the crisis has passed, as the experience of World War I, the Great Depression, and World War II shows. National defense is a primary function of government, and reasonable tax increases for legitimate emergencies are not unwarranted. Implementing political devices that ensure that war taxes end when the war does would protect long-term justice and economic well being. For instance, this could be accomplished by sunset clauses, in other words, by writing into the war tax law in question an automatic expiration within a specific period of time after hostilities cease.

Taxes should be visible as well. As under any truly just system of government, people know the laws to which they are bound, so should they know what the tax laws are requiring them to pay. This means avoiding income tax withholding, separate employer-paid payroll taxes, and taxes whose cost is buried in the price of goods and services, such as the gasoline excise tax. As Adam Smith wrote in *The Wealth of Nations*:

> The tax which each individual is bound to pay ought to be certain, and not arbitrary. The time of payment, the manner of payment, the quantity to be paid, ought to be clear and plain to the contributor. . . . Where it is otherwise, every person subject to the tax is put more or less in the power of the tax-gatherer, who can either aggravate the tax upon any obnoxious uncertainty, or extort, by the terror of such aggravation, some present or perquisite to himself. The uncertainty of taxation encourages the insolence and favours the corruption of an order of men who are naturally unpopular . . .[1]

The IRS, or any other agency charged with enforcing tax law, should be: bound by the demands of due process, required to follow its own rules, and prohibited from intimidating or harassing citizens. Penalties for violating tax law should be commensurate with the gravity of the offense.

All these measures will greatly enhance the tax code's comprehensibility. Restoring understandability will help restore western justice to tax enforcement. The code should be simple enough that honest people of common intelligence can be sure that they have not broken the law.

Starving Leviathan

Because taxes enable spending and spending enshrines taxes, criteria for appropriate spending are also important.

The twentieth century attests to the fact that it is the nature of government to grow and accumulate power. The Constitution should protect against this tendency. While it is not a perfect document, and can be changed according to the proper procedure, it should never be ignored, deemed irrelevant, or viewed as an obstacle to progress. Spending programs should be evaluated first to determine whether or not they are Constitutional. This used to be the norm. As James Beck, former solicitor general of the United States, points out:

> In the days of Webster, Clay, and Calhoun, the constitutionality of any proposed statute might be debated for days and even weeks, but not so at the present time. In the House a few hours at most, to be divided in ten or twenty minute intervals between supporters and defenders of the legislation, are set aside for such debate and a member cannot even develop his theme, much less intelligently debate it, in such a short period of time. Also, the burden of committee work is such that for weeks a member of an important [c]ommittee may be unable to do more than appear on the floor for a short time. The remainder of his time and energy must be devoted to hearing arguments of the bureaucracy and its supporters or opponents for additional grants of public money or for further surrenders of legislative authority and jurisdiction.[2]

Constitutional adherence is especially vital during times of crisis. As Justice Mahlon Pitney declared, "[A]n emergency can neither create a power nor excuse a defiance of the limitations upon the powers of the Government."[3] Operating in crisis mode, with no regard to long-term consequences, perpetuates crisis. Creating policies in response to immediate concerns rather than according to transcendent principle saddles future generations with outdated and inappropriate policies that can do more harm than good.

The government should spend no more than it is taking in. To do otherwise is to: remove a natural check on the growth of the government, make tax increases necessary later on, and burden following generations with debt that they did not assume. Conversely, it should return surpluses immediately to the people who earned them. History shows that unreturned surpluses are quickly spent away. Thus it is important that they be returned immediately to avoid expanding the government even further and making future taxes necessary.

The logical results of any spending policy should be carefully considered in the light of human depravity. What is unthinkable in one generation can become the norm in the next when federal incentives are involved. Programs should not foster social breakdown by rewarding vice or promoting dependency or funding outright evil, such as abortion, contraception for unmarried minors, and pornography. Though fundamentally dangerous in and of themselves, these outrages are made more so by the fact that they perpetuate themselves and create others. They also reduce many of their benefactors to moral slavery by plundering them to fund that which they deem morally reprehensible.

Federal programs should not usurp responsibility belonging to the family. Expecting and allowing government to provide what has traditionally fallen under the purview of the family unavoidably increases the power of government while diminishing the autonomy of the family. Ironically, this denigration of the family and the social devastation that it produces leads to cries for more government intervention. This is not the solution. The answer to the problems caused by excessive government is less government, not more.

The simultaneous weakening of the family and growth of government of the last century recall the damaging effects of the drug plague. They have: been addictive, numbed the nation morally and mentally, been economically expensive, and reduced the family to a state of dependency. The first step in kicking the habit will be to start thinking policies through before approving and implementing them. They should be supported or opposed for reasons that are deeper than whether or not they are superficially appealing. For instance, some questions to ask are:

- What does the Constitution say?
- What are some possible unintended consequences? Will it weaken the family or religious institutions? Does it promote dependency,

laziness, covetousness, etc.? Does it make immoral behavior easier/ attractive? Does it appeal to human depravity? Does it erode respect for the family? Does it teach the wrong moral lessons?

- Does it pervert justice?
- Is it real tax reform or just tinkering? Will it increase or decrease complexity?
- Is it impartial? Is it simple? Is it transparent?
- Is it a proper function of government? Is it a good idea? Can the government really do it well? What is its track record in similar areas? Could/should the family or church do it better?
- Does it inhibit economic growth?
- Is the government likely to keep its promises?
- Will it expand the power of the state? Does it set up a new state apparatus that could be dangerous sooner or later?
- Will it erode privacy, financial or otherwise?
- Is it the best solution or just the quickest fix?

The history of federal tax and spending policies is the history of secondary consequences. While many of these consequences have been economic, others are moral. The failure to think policies and their consequences through, weigh them against the Constitution, and look for more suitable options has borne the fruit of economic loss, family and social breakdown, and moral crisis. Learning from the lessons of the past will aid in correcting the problems of the present and preventing their recurrence in the future.

Section VI

FIFTEEN

Tax Reform Plans

In 1999, *Tax Notes* published a copy of a satirical memo reportedly circulated by Treasury Department economists. The memo heralded the creation of the "None of the Above Credit," a new tax credit available to "taxpayers who are not eligible for any of the existing tax credits." As the memo explained, "The proposed tax credit is carefully targeted at that underserved group, and has been found to be popular in focus groups."[1]

As the joke memo highlights, making tax policy by tinkering has reached absurd proportions. The problems with our tax code have become so overwhelming that the only real solution is to eliminate it and start from scratch. Piecemeal tax cuts are not enough. It is time for ambitious tax relief that both simplifies the tax structure and significantly cuts Americans' tax bills.

A number of solutions have been proposed to end America's tax nightmare. While none of the current ideas for fundamental tax reform is perfect, they would bring vast improvements over current tax law. All serious proposals will substantially reduce the damage wrought by current tax policy. This chapter describes the major ideas and explores the advantages and disadvantages of each. It also introduces some less sweeping, shorter-term proposals.

Income Tax Reform

FLAT INCOME TAX
In contrast to our current, graduated income tax, a flat income tax would tax income only once and at one rate. For instance, under a representative plan, all taxable income would be taxed at 17 percent, instead of climbing

through several different rates. Income could be taxed only after an individual or family has passed a certain exemption level; most current plans exempt about $35,000 for a family of four. In other words, a family of four would pay no income tax on earnings up to $35,000; they would pay the flat rate only on earnings above that amount. For example, assuming an exemption of $35,000 and a 17 percent flat rate, a family of four earning $40,000 would pay $850 in federal income taxes [($40,000-$35,000) x 17%].

Under most plans, individuals would not pay investment taxes directly; investment income would be taxed only once at the corporate level. This means that businesses would pay the income tax on their earnings and then pass after-tax dollars on to their investors in the form of dividends. Since these earnings will already have been taxed, investors will not have to pay further taxes on them.

Under a pure flat tax system, there would be no deductions or credits. Modified flat tax plans allow for a few deductions, such as charitable contributions. Either way, the current code's morass of loopholes would be eliminated.

Such a plan is vastly preferable to the present system. In addition to imposing a lower tax rate, it will eliminate the multiple taxation of investment income. There will be no bracket creep; workers will not be forced into higher tax brackets for earning more money. This means that workers and their families, not the government, will benefit most from their hard work and success. This will help restore family autonomy, allowing families more economic freedom to meet their own needs, set their own priorities, and achieve their own goals.

A flat income tax would also diminish the perverse moral lessons taught by the discouragement of hard work and good stewardship. It would promote economic growth; there would be more capital, more jobs, higher wages, higher savings. Estimates vary, but reliable sources project that the economy would grow 0.5 to 1 percent higher for several years following enactment of a flat tax. According to The Heritage Foundation, growth of just 0.5 percent each year for ten years would add $5,000 to an average family of four's income.[2] According to Dale Jorgenson, chairman of the economics department at Harvard, enactment of a flat tax would immediately boost wealth by $1 trillion.[3] This is because the value of financial assets is determined by the after-tax income they generate. Reducing taxes and eliminating multiple layers of taxation boosts after-tax income. This too will increase family freedom by creating more job opportunities and higher wages.

A flat income tax would be much simpler than the present labyrinth. Instead of the pages and pages of forms under the current system, most taxpayers would be able to file their returns on a form no bigger than a postcard. The complicated morass of deductions and credits would be eliminated, as would the alternative minimum tax. This means that compliance costs will be lower and preparing taxes will be less time-consuming. Families will benefit because they will no longer have to sacrifice time together to prepare tax forms or pay someone else to perform the task for them. Because it will be simple and understandable, honest citizens will be able to know that they haven't broken the law. This will protect them against the bully tactics of the IRS, which will lose much of its freedom to interpret the tax laws its own way.

A flat income tax would honor the American concept of justice and equality before the law. All Americans will be treated equally, subject to one tax rate. This will end the current code's punitive treatment of marriage. It would also short circuit campaigns to raise or lower taxes on some groups but not others. Instead of pitting one group of taxpayers against another, any tax hike or cut would reach everybody. This will make it harder to raise taxes. It will also reduce the power of special interest groups lobbying for favors in the tax code.

Families will enjoy greater moral freedom. Lower taxes will leave them more money and thus more freedom of choice. Instead of guiding citizens into state-sanctioned behaviors and lifestyles, the greater neutrality of the tax code will free them to make decisions on their own and not force them into choosing among evils.

While a flat income tax would be a vast improvement over the current system, it is imperfect. First of all, it is still an income tax, meaning that it discourages earning income. While this problem is greatly improved by the elimination of graduated marginal rates, the fundamental punitive treatment of income remains. Moreover, since most realistic plans call for an exempt level of income, they would not fully eliminate progressivity from the tax system. Additionally, such a system would still violate citizens' privacy by forcing them to reveal the sources and amounts of some income, although they would no longer have to open all their assets to federal scrutiny.

Another problem is that federal revenues are actually expected to increase under many proposals. This is because the reduction of perverse incentives creates economic growth, meaning higher economic output, which can be taxed. As explained earlier, this is what happened under the Kennedy and Reagan tax cuts. For this reason, the lowest possible tax rate should be adopted, to prevent government from receiving any additional revenues, especially in times of surplus. In addition, the law should include a provision to lower taxes automatically if revenues increase.

NATIONAL SALES TAX

Another option for replacing the current federal income tax, and possibly the payroll and other taxes as well, is a national sales tax, similar to those imposed by many states. The national sales tax would be levied on final goods and services at purchase. For example, if a consumer purchases a book, he would be charged a national sales tax on the book when he purchased it. In order to keep the national sales tax from being regressive (in other words, from disproportionately afflicting low-income families), many plans call for exempting approximately $20,000 in income for a family of four from the sales tax. One exciting consumption tax proposal, called the Fair Tax, would replace the individual income tax, the alternative minimum tax, corporate and business income taxes, capital gains taxes, the self-employment tax, estate and gift taxes, and all payroll taxes, including the Social Security and Medicare taxes.

Like the flat income tax, this approach would lower taxes. Instead of punishing earning, saving, and investing, a national sales tax would discourage consumption. This means that families will no longer be discouraged from responsible economic behavior. Dale Jorgenson calculates that a flat-rate consumption-based tax that raises as much revenue as the current complex income tax would increase economic growth by more than $200 billion. That means that a fairer, simpler system that raises the same amount of revenue as the current one would raise average household income by $2,000 annually.[4] It would respect privacy far more than any form of income tax, as Americans would not be forced to reveal their income and its sources.

A national sales tax would be more voluntary than the income tax. Under the current system, taxpayers must view earning opportunities through the lens of their tax consequences. Under a sales tax, they would view consumption the same way. As reducing personal consumption has far fewer negative effects than reducing personal income, taxpayers would have more control.

It would be much simpler than the current system. Special interest lobbies that benefit from preferences under the current system would lose power. Compliance costs would be greatly reduced. According to The Tax Foundation, a national sales tax would lower compliance costs for businesses and workers by more than 90 percent. That is the equivalent of adding $1,000–2,500 to the income of every household in the United States.[5] Most individuals would not have to file tax returns, and the IRS could be abolished. This will save families time and expense, and relieve them from the fear of IRS bullying tactics.

Many of the moral advantages to a sales tax also mirror those of a flat income tax, including stopping the discouragement of responsible behavior, eliminating the marriage penalty, and ceasing the encouragement of envy. It would also echo the virtues that make a healthy society while retreating from the moral decision-making process.

Like the flat income tax, the national sales tax has disadvantages. It too brings the risk of increased federal revenues. It could also be dangerous to implement without repealing the sixteenth amendment, as Americans could victimized by both income and sales taxes.[6]

VALUE-ADDED TAX

A value-added tax (VAT) is a kind of sales tax common in Europe. *Value added* is typically defined as gross receipts from sales less purchases from other businesses, in other words, the amount of monetary value that each business that refines a product adds to it. A value-added tax is levied at each stage of production performed by a different firm. Consider shoes as an example. First, a hunter kills an animal. He sells the hide to a tanner, who converts it into leather. The tanner sells the leather to a cobbler. The cobbler sells the manufactured shoes to a store. The store sells them to customers. At each stage, value has been added to the product. (You're willing to pay more for a finished pair of shoes than for a raw hide.) That added value, the difference between the value of the product at purchase and at resale, is what is taxed.

Although it shares many of the advantages of the national sales tax, the VAT has been disastrous in Europe. As a hidden tax, it is easy to raise, and has continually increased. Its complicated nature expands government and makes it expensive to administer.

A VAT forces businesses to bear heavy compliance costs in order to serve as tax collectors for the government. Exempting certain goods, such as necessities like food, exacerbates this problem, as firms have to segregate records according to tax status and submit multiple separate forms to the government. Moreover, most countries with VATs not only exempt certain goods, but also apply different tax rates to different products. In some countries, there are as many as six separate tax rates.[7] Such complexity disproportionately hurts the small businesses on which many families depend and which create the most jobs. Canada's VAT is estimated to have driven one-fourth of small businesses into the underground economy within two years of its adoption in 1991.[8]

Payroll Tax Reform

The complex problems of the Social Security system make real payroll tax reform difficult. While the system is going bankrupt, many Americans believe that some sort of commitment exists to continue to transfer the earnings of workers to the retired, despite the fact that the Supreme Court stated categorically that workers do not have any accrued property rights associated with the system nor do they have any legal claim to accrued tax payments or anticipated benefits in *Fleming v. Nestor* (1960).[9] Because of this mistaken idea, no serious proposals for fully eliminating the program exist.

Privatization

However, because it is well recognized that the current structure is untenable, a number of reform proposals have been advanced. The most commonly discussed is privatization. Privatization means allowing workers to invest what they now pay in payroll taxes in their own personal accounts. Privatization could be full or partial. This means that either all or a portion of the money that workers currently lose in payroll taxes could be diverted into their private retirement accounts. Most current proposals call for partial privatization, with the current Social Security structure remaining but paying lower benefits. Milton Friedman points out that the system could be privatized and remaining "commitments" covered via other taxes, permitting repeal of the Social Security portion of the payroll tax.[10]

Such a system would give families much more control. They could choose their own investments and almost be certain of a higher return than what they would receive under the current system. According to The Heritage Foundation, many workers would reap more than twice what they can expect under the current Social Security system.[11] In addition, they would be protected from government-imposed benefit cuts.

According to economist Peter Ferrera of Americans for Tax Reform, privatization "would open up a whole new realm of prosperity for working people in America. . . . [I]t would ultimately produce the greatest reduction in government taxes, spending and debt in world history."[12]

Further, partial privatization would create competition between Social Security and the private market, allowing workers to compare Social Security's paltry return with the market's historically higher one and could thus create a groundswell of support for complete privatization. Moreover, giving families direct control of their savings affirms the idea that primary responsibility for the future lies with the family, not the government.

Estate Tax Reform

Unlike with the income tax, there is really only one serious proposal for reforming the estate tax: eliminating it quickly and permanently. (The much celebrated estate tax repeal contained in the 2001 tax cut does not fully materialize until 2010 and then lasts only for that one year.) While many flat income and national sales tax plans include eliminating the estate tax, the tax on dying could be eliminated by itself. Terminating the estate tax would help families by increasing economic growth. An Institute for Policy Innovation study found that eliminating the estate tax in 1999 would, by 2010, have:

- Increased annual gross domestic product by $117.3 billion or .9 percent
- Increased U.S. capital stock by $1.5 trillion or 4.1 percent
- Created 236,000 additional jobs[13]

With the elimination of the estate tax, punitive treatment of saving and investing would also be eliminated. Repeal would protect small businesses and family farms from being forced out of business by the tax. It would eliminate one of many layers of taxation. It would also end the costs of complying with the tax; this would especially help small and medium-sized businesses. Strengthening small farms and businesses would strengthen the many families who depend on them. It would end the discouragement of the noble goal of providing for one's family after death. The only real disadvantage to eliminating the estate tax is that the greater economic growth might result in an increase in federal revenues.

Sort-Term Solutions

In addition to the above major proposals for tax reform, there are several less sweeping ideas that should be considered in the short term:

Balanced Budget Amendment

A Constitutional amendment to require a balanced federal budget and limit increases in federal spending to the rate of economic growth or less would hold spending down and provide incentive to avoid growth-killing taxes.

ALTERNATIVE MAXIMUM TAX

This idea was first proposed by Steve Moore of the Club for Growth. It would allow taxpayers to choose between the current system and an alternative federal tax that would take only 25 percent of their income between both payroll and income taxes. This would give middle-class families a break from the dual tax structure that forces them to pay higher combined marginal rates than the wealthy. By giving taxpayers a choice without forcing them to give up deductions, such a move would undercut the rich special-interest lobbies fighting to keep the current code. Such an approach is not unprecedented; an optional flat tax has already worked well in Hong Kong, giving workers a choice between a 15 percent flat rate and a complex system like ours, and rendering the latter obsolete.[14]

END WITHHOLDING

Ending tax withholding would increase the visibility of the income tax by requiring workers to pay it directly, rather than have it taken out of their paychecks. This would end the immoral practice of forcing workers to give the government an interest-free loan. It would make income and payroll taxes more visible, making clearer to citizens how much they're paying and better enabling them to judge whether government is worth the price.

SUPERMAJORITY

This proposal would make it harder to raise taxes by requiring a two-thirds majority of both houses of Congress to implement increases. While it would still be possible to raise taxes, increases would require broad support. The four largest tax hikes since 1980—in 1982, 1983, 1990, and 1993—would have failed under this rule.[15] The experience of states with supermajority requirements shows that they work well. Such states tax less, spend less, enjoy greater economic growth, and create more jobs.[16]

SUNSETS

Daniel Mitchell of The Heritage Foundation has proposed passing legislation terminating the tax code by a certain date. This would force Congress to come up with an alternative system or forgo revenue. The idea has worked well in states that have tried it. Another idea is to sunset all tax increases, in other words, enact them on a temporary basis scheduled to terminate on a specific date.

DEDUCT PAYROLL TAXES FROM TAXABLE INCOME

Making payroll taxes deductible under the federal income tax, as state and local taxes are now. This would end one form of double taxation.

MORAL HAZARD STATEMENT

Impact statements are analyses of how proposed policy changes are likely to affect something of concern. For instance, a Family Impact Statement addresses the effect of a particular policy on the family. A Moral Hazard Statement would highlight any perverse moral incentives created by changes in fiscal policy. Preparing such a statement could be the work of a commission on the moral impact of fiscal policy, which might comprise ethicists and economists working together to study such effects.

NO NEW TAXES

From time to time, proposals for new taxes come forward. Given the government's record of irresponsibility with the money that it already takes, there is no justification for any new taxes.

There are probably as many ideas for tax reform as there are taxpayers. One thing that virtually all can agree on, though, is that all taxpayers need and deserve fundamental tax reform that will lower the tax burden and simplify the tax rules and restore justice to the tax system.

This great nation was not founded to confiscate one-third of family income, to impose a massive welfare state, and thereby slowly bleed itself of virtue and valor. It was founded as a land of freedom and opportunity, where government existed to protect and defend the people and their rights so that they can provide for themselves and live as they believe best. It is time to restore that vision to our tax system.

SIXTEEN

Conclusion

Today's America is in moral peril. Forced to surrender high amounts of their income to the government, the people have become increasingly dependent as the state has grown more powerful. Each time they turn to government for help, they legitimize it as their provider, until they become enslaved and the noblest form of government yet conceived is turned into a kind of overbearing cash machine.

At the same time, the citizens' personal character is compromised. This diminution of personal character begins on the tax side of fiscal policy. The law is a teacher; public policy that eschews wisdom, perverts justice, and undermines righteousness teaches the rejection of these virtues. Hence the people become confused; neither right nor wrong seems clear any longer. From saving less and spending more to even rejecting marriage, Americans respond to their tax structure and its perverse incentives by choosing behavior that is morally and economically bad for the nation and its families.

Having begun with perverse tax policy, the slow corrosion of character accelerates with the consequent transformation of government from protector of rights to provider of goodies. Citizens debase themselves by viewing the government as some kind of omnipresent benefactor of first resort, rather than a God-ordained institution limited to the defined but vital role of safeguarding rights so that they can enjoy equal opportunity to provide for themselves and their own. Also debased is family as the government usurps its role, weakening this vital institution and in turn society as a whole, leaving both ill-equipped to undo the damage done by government when it seeks to fill functions for which it is neither intended nor equipped.

Such an outcome only enshrines the ever-growing dependency that has left many only vaguely aware that they are responsible for their own lives and families. Ever-louder grow the cries for more government help in situations that used to be regarded as the proper purview of the individual, the family, or religious institutions. The pursuit of protection not from violations of rights but rather from the difficulties and unpredictability of life has created a victim mentality, wherein no one is capable of taking care of himself and everyone is entitled to provision from the government, which really means from his fellow citizens.

All this moral damage is being wrought in pursuit of something that cannot work. People working together in the natural order yield prosperity. Government has been established to protect rights whose exercise creates wealth. When government instead violates those rights in order to redistribute wealth, it destroys the very thing it purports to spread.

Ironically, though government becomes more powerful through gradual encroachments, it too is debased. Conceived as the guardian of liberty of a free people, the U.S. Constitutional government has been perverted into a battle ground for special interest groups each seeking its supposed "fair share." Having moved from the role of protecting rights to providing every need from childcare to Medicare, it demeans liberty and opportunity and, along with them, itself as their guardian and protector.

But the people are starting to fight back. In late 2008, a plumber named Joe Wurzelbacher became a media sensation when he challenged then-Sen. Barack Obama on the injustice of his plans for wealth redistribution. At a campaign rally, Mr. Wurzelbacher explained that he'd worked hard to build his plumbing business, and that Mr. Obama's plan would raise his taxes.

Sen. Obama responded: "I think when you spread the wealth around it's good for everybody."

Mr. Wurzelbacher didn't buy it, and neither do millions of Americans who work hard and resent having their government mock their sacrifices by spreading the fruits of their of labor and responsibility to others.

America's tax policy has created a moral crisis no less severe than that spawned by the Stamp Act more than 200 years ago. Meeting this moral crisis will take time and commitment. It will require restoring proper expectations of government and doing the hard work of thinking through policy solutions instead of giving in to the enticements of resentment. It will require a firm commitment to designing a new tax structure according the vision of the morally strong nation that the United States can be again. And it will require the resolve of the true heirs to the Revolution, the ones willing to buck the soft despotism of wealth redistribution, the ones who know where the country must go, the ones who won't be held hostage in Omelas.

NOTES

Introduction

1. Jim Yardley, "A Shy Child's Journey to Fiery Mass Murder," *International Herald Tribune*, October 11, 2001.
2. Lisa Beyer, "Roots of Rage," *Time*, October 1, 2001, 46.
3. John Cloud, "Atta's Odyssey," *Time*, October 8, 2001, 65.
4. Henry Wadsworth Longfellow, *Evangeline: A Tale of Arcadia*, 1847.

ONE. A Vision for Fiscal Reform

1. J.M. Thompson, *The French Revolution* (Stroud, UK: Sutton Publishing, 2002), 117.

TWO. Taxes and Revolution

1. Bernard Bailyn, *The Origins of American Politics* (New York: Vintage Books, 1970), 56.
2. Quoted in Charles Adams, *Those Dirty Rotten Taxes: The Tax Revolts that Built America* (New York: The Free Press, 1998), 35.
3. John Phillip Reid, *Constitutional History of the American Revolution: The Authority to Tax* (Madison, WI: University of Wisconsin Press, 1987), 88.
4. Reid, *Constitutional History*, 145, quoted in Adams, *For Good and Evil*, 280.
5. John Phillip Reid, *The Concept of Liberty in the Age of the American Revolution* (Chicago: University of Chicago Press, 1988), 53, quoted in James Bovard, *Freedom in Chains: The Rise of the State and the Demise of the Citizen* (New York: St. Martin's Press, 1999), 202.
5. Marvin Olasky, *Fighting for Liberty and Virtue: Political and Culture Wars in Eighteenth-Century America* (Wheaton, IL: Crossway Books, 1995), 126.
6. Carl Bridenbaugh, *Mitre and Sceptre* (Oxford: Oxford University Press, 1967), 237, quoted in Olasky, *Fighting for Liberty and Virtue*, 126.
7. Samuel Adams, *The Writings of Samuel Adams*, vol. 2 (Charleston: Bibliobazaar, 2007), 232, quoted in Olasky, *Fighting for Liberty and Virtue*, 126.
8. James Otis, "A Man's House is His Castle," published in *Our Nation's Archive: The History of the United States in Documents*, ed. Erik Bruun and Jay Crosby (New York: Black Dog & Levanthal Publishers, 1999), 101. Note: No known

written text of Otis's remarks exists; this account is based on notes taken by John Adams, who heard Otis speak.

9. John Dickinson, *Letter from A Farmer In Pennsylvania To the Inhabitants of the British Colonies* (Temecula, CA: Reprint Services Corp, 1903).

10. Quoted in Thomas P. Slaughter, *The Whiskey Rebellion: Frontier Epilogue to the American Revolution* (Oxford: Oxford University Press, 1986), 128.

11. *The Philadelphia Resolutions* 2, 6 (October 16, 1773), http://avalon.law.yale.edu/18th_century/phil_res_1772.asp

12. George Washington, letter to George William Fairfax, June 10, 1774.

13. *Journals of the Continental Congress, 1774–1789*, Cont. Cong., October 14, 1774, 64.

14. Ibid., 67.

15. Ibid., 68.

THREE. **A Newborn Nation**

1. Alexander Hamilton, *The Continentalist* VI (July 4, 1782).

2. *The Continentalist* IV (August 30, 1781).

3. Richard Brookhiser, *Alexander Hamilton, American* (New York: Simon & Schuster, 2000), 54.

4. Forrest McDonald, *E Pluribus Unum: The Formation of the American Republic 1776–1790*, Second Edition (Indianapolis: LibertyPress, 1979), 244–55.

5. Edmund S. Morgan, *The Meaning of Independence: John Adams, George Washington, and Thomas Jefferson* (Richmond: University of Virginia Press, 1976), 47.

6. Brookhiser, *Alexander Hamilton*, 60.

7. Some argue that Isaiah 33:22 was the original source of the separation of powers: "[T]he LORD is our judge, The LORD is our lawgiver, The LORD is our King."

8. Quotations from the Constitutional debates are taken from James Madison's *Notes of Debates in the Federal Convention of 1787*.

9. U.S. Constitution, art. VI.

10. U.S. Constitution, art. I, sec. 8.

11. Thomas M. Cooley, A Treatise on the Law of Taxation, (Chicago: Callahan and Company, 1876), 3.

12. Samuel Johnson, *A Dictionary of the English Language* (London: Richard Bentley, 1755).

13. U.S. Constitution, art. I, sec 9.

14. Charles de Secondat Montesquieu, *The Spirit of the Laws*, Third Edition (The Colonial Press, 1900), 215.

15. U.S. Constitution, art. I, sec. 9.

FOUR. **Early Quarrels**

1. In Congress, April 9, 1789

2. Orrin Leslie Elliot, *The Tariff Controversy in the United States, 1789–1833* (Palo Alto, CA: University of California, 1892), 67.

3. Elliott, *The Tariff Controversy*, 91.

4. Alexander Hamilton, *Opinion as to the Constitutionality of the Bank of the United States*, (Whitefish, MT: Kessinger Publishing, 1791).

5. James Madison, speech in congress Opposing National Bank, Feb. 2, 1791.
6. Hamilton, Alexander, *Report on the Subject of Manufactures, Made in his Capacity of Secretary of the Treasury* (Whitefish, MT: Kessinger Publishing, 1791).
7. *The First Report on Public Credit* (January 9, 1970).
8. Charles Adams, *Those Dirty Rotten Taxes,* 66.
9. Brenda Yelvington, "Excise Taxes in Historical Perspective," in *Taxing Choice,* ed. William F. Shughart (Oakland, CA: The Independent Institute, 1997), 34.
10. Charles Adams, *For Good and Evil,* 317.
11. William F. Shughart II, ed., *Taxing Choice: The Predatory Politics of Fiscal Discrimination* (Oakland, CA: The Independent Institute, 1997), 34.
12. Charles Adams, *Those Dirty Rotten Taxes,* 67.
13. Ibid.
14. Ibid., 67–68.
15. Ibid., 68.
16. Yelvington, *Excise Taxes,* 34–35.
17. Quoted in Amity Shlaes, *The Greedy Hand: How Taxes Drive Americans Crazy and What to Do about It* (New York: Random House, 1999), 40.
18. Quoted in Shlaes, *The Greedy Hand,* 40.
19. William Findley, "Whiskey Rebellion," *Our Nation's Archive,* 188.
20. Adam Gifford, Jr. "Whiskey, Margarine, and Newspapers: A Tale of Three Taxes," in Shughart, *Taxing Choice,* 63.
21. Yelvington, *Excise Tax,* 35–36.
22. Shughart, *Taxing Choice,* 36–37.
23. Richard Wiggington Thompson, *The History of Protective Tariff Laws,* Third Edition (Chicago: R. S. Peale & Co. 1888), 118–28.
24. Paul F. Boller, *Presidential Campaigns: from George Washington to George W. Bush,* Second Edition (Oxford: Oxford University Press, 2004), 32–37.
25. John Quincy Adams, Message to Congress, 1825.
26. Thomas Jefferson, Letter to William B. Giles, Dec. 26, 1825.
27. Thompson, *The History,* 164.
28. William W. Freehling, *Prelude to Civil War: the Nullification Controversy in South Carolina, 1816–1836* (Oxford: Oxford University Press, 1992), 125.
29. Taussig, 88–89.
30. Taussig, 100.
31. Taussig, 101.
32. Freehling, *Prelude,* 158–59.
33. M. J. Heale, *The Making of American Politics* (New York: Longman, 1977), 165.
34. Arthur M. Schlesinger, Jr., *The Age of Jackson* (New York: Little, Brown, and Company, 1945), 95.
35. Schlesinger, *The Age of Jackson,* 95–96.

FIVE. **The Income Tax versus the Constitution**

1. Sheldon D. Pollack, *The Failure of U.S. Tax Policy: Revenue and Politics* (New York: Penguin Books, 1996), 41.
2. Yelvington, *Excise Tax,* 37.
3. Pollack, *The Failure of U.S. Tax Policy,* 42.
4. Max West, *The Inheritance Tax,* Second Edition (New York: Columbia University Press, 1908), 89.

5. Shughart, *Taxing Choice*, 37.

6. Pollack, *The Failure of U.S. Tax Policy*, 43.

7. Shughart, *Taxing Choice*, 37.

8. David B. Levenstam, "Constitutional Challenge: Repealing the 16th Amendment wouldn't kill the income tax," *Reason* (January 1999).

9. John F. Witte, *The Politics and Development of the Federal Income Tax* (London: The University of Wisconsin Press, Ltd., 1985), 70.

10. Robert Higgs, *Crisis and Leviathan: Critical Episodes in the Growth of American Government* (Oxford: Oxford University Press, 1987), 113–14.

11. Charles R. Kessler, ed., *The Federalist Papers* (New York: Signet Classics, 2003).

12. Higgs, *Crisis and Leviathan*, 113–14.

13. Quoted in Arthur M. Schlesinger, Jr., "The New Freedom Fulfills the New Nationalism," in *The Progressive Era: Liberal Renaissance or Liberal Failure?* ed. Arthur Mann (Austin: Holt, Rinehart and Winston, 1963), 59.

14. Schlesinger, "New Freedom Fulfils the New Nationalism," 59.

15. Quoted in Edward J. Erler, "The Progessive Income Tax and the Progressive Attack on the Founding," The Claremont Institute (June 1, 1998), http://www.claremont.org.

16. Quoted in Erler, "The Progressive Income Tax."

17. Robert Stanley, *Dimensions of Law in the Service of Order.* (Oxford: Oxford University Press, 1993), 118–19.

18. Quoted in Arnold M. Paul, *Conservative Crisis and the Rule of Law: Attitudes of Bar and Bench, 1877–1895* (New York: Harper & Row, 1969).

19. Charles Adams, *Those Dirty Rotten Taxes*, 147.

20. *Pollock v. Farmers' Loan & Trust Co.*, 157 U.S. 429 (1895).

21. Ibid.

22. *Pollock v. Farmers' Loan & Trust Co.*, 157 U.S. 429, 596 (1895).

23. *Pollock v. Farmers' Loan & Trust Co.*, 157 U.S. 607 (1895).

24. Ibid.

25. *Knowlton v. Moore* 178 U.S. 41, 109 (1899).

26. Higgs, *Crisis and Leviathan*, 110.

27. Ecenbarger, "Many Unhappy Returns."

28. Charles Adams, *For Good and Evil*, 364.

29. Quoted in Erler, "The Progressive Income Tax." Lee Benson, in his book *Turner & Beard*, argues that Beard derived his ideas largely from Achilla Loria, an Italian economist who borrowed from Marx.

30. Witte, *The Politics and Development*, 78.

31. Ecenbarger, "Many Unhappy Returns."

SIX. **The Century of Taxes**

1. Gary Robbins and Aldona Robbins, "The Case for Burying the Estate Tax," Institute for Policy Innovation, *Policy Report*, no. 150 (March 15, 1999): 3.

2. Daniel J. Mitchell, "The Historical Lessons of Lower Tax Rates," The Heritage Foundation, *Backgrounder*, no. 1086 (July 19, 1996): 3.

3. *Bromley v. McCaughn*, 280 U.S. 124 (1929).

4. E. Cary Brown, "Fiscal Policy in the Thirties: A Reappraisal," *American Economic Review* 46, no. 5 (December 1956): 869.

5. Brown, "Fiscal Policy," 869.
6. Schlesinger, *The Progressive Era*, 325–26, quoted in Bruce Bartlett, "Debt Not Rising Precipitously," National Center for Policy Analysis, *Opinion Editorial* (January 17, 2000), http://www.ncpa.org/oped/bartlett/jan1700.html.
7. Mitchell, "The Historical Lessons of Lower Tax Rates," 6.
8. Gary Robbins and Aldona Robbins, "A Tax Deduction for Payroll Taxes: An Analysis of the Ashcroft Proposal," Institute for Policy Innovation, *Policy Reports*, no. 142 (June 1997).
9. A. Haeworth Robertson, *The Coming Revolution in Social Security* (Reston, VA: Reston Publishing Company, 1981), 73.
10. Robbins and Robbins, "A Tax Deduction for Payroll Taxes."
11. Gary Robbins and Aldona Robbins, "Reducing the Marriage Penalty: A Good Way to Cut Taxes?" Institute for Policy Innovation, *Issue Brief* (July 15, 1998): 7.
12. Ibid.
13. Samuel I. Rosenman, ed., *The Public Papers and Addresses of Franklin D. Roosevelt* (New York: Harper & Brothers, 1950), 90.
14. Mark Leff, *The Limits of Symbolic Reform: The New Deal and Taxation, 1933–1939* (London: Cambridge University Press, 1984), 290–91.
15. Ecenbarger, "Many Unhappy Returns."
16. Robertson, *The Coming Revolution*, 73.
17. Gerald W. Scully, "Measuring the Burden of High Taxes," National Center for Policy Analysis, July 1, 1998.
18. John F. Kennedy, speech to Economic Club of New York, December 14, 1962.
19. Mitchell, "The Historical Lessons of Lower Tax Rates," 4.
20. John A. Andrew III, *Lyndon Johnson and the Great Society* (Chicago: Ivan R. Dee Publisher, 1998), 15.
21. Robbins and Robbins, "The Case for Burying the Estate Tax," Institute for Policy Innovation, *Policy Report* 150 (March 15, 1999): 5.
22. Ibid, 5–7.
23. Ibid, 7.
24. Ibid.
25. Ibid., 5.
26. Mitchell, "The Historical Lessons of Lower Tax Rates," 5.
27. Ibid., 6.
28. NYSSCPA's Testimony at Finance Hearing on IRS, "Treatment of Taxpayers," *Tax Notes Today*, Sept. 24, 1997.

SEVEN. **Taxes in the Twenty-First Century**

1. Josh Barro, "America Celebrates Tax Freedom Day", Tax Foundation, *Special Report 165*, April 2009.
2. Ibid.
3. "America to Celebrate Tax Freedom Day on May 3, 2001," Tax Foundation, April 13, 2001. http://www.taxfoundation.org/taxfreedomday.html.
4. Barro, "America Celebrates."
5. "America to Celebrate Tax Freedom Day on May 3, 2001," Tax Foundation.
6. *Source:* http://www.taxfoundation.org/UserFiles/Image/Tax-Freedom-Day/2008/figure4large.jpg.

7. Stephen Moore, "Congress's Tax Cut Imperative," Cato Institute (June 17, 1998), http://www.cato.org/pub_display.php?pub_id=5683.
8. Andrew Chamberlain and Gerald Prante, "Which Taxes Weigh Most Heavily on Americans with Different Incomes?" Tax Foundation, *Fiscal Facts*, March 26, 2007.
9. "Five Principles of Social Security Reform," National Center for Policy Analysis, *Brief Analysis*, no. 302 (July 26, 1999): 2.
10. "A New Framework for Cutting Taxes: Reforming the Tax Code and Improving Social Security," The Heritage Foundation, *Backgrounder*, no. 1199 (July 1, 1998): 9–10.
11. Robbins and Robbins, "The Case for Burying the Estate Tax", p. 17.
12. Ibid., 18.
13. David Orenstein, "It's called an unfair tax on death, but advocates say it serves a social purpose," *The* (Albany) *Times Union*, March 29, 1998, C1.

EIGHT. **Destroying Justice in the Name of Fairness**

1. "Irritated at Income Tax? Think of it as Tradition," *The Plain Dealer*, March 23, 1998, 4C
2. Aristotle, *The Politics*, Book III, Ch. x, trans. Thomas Alan Sinclair, Trevor J. Saunders (New York: Penguin Classics, 1981).
3. "Irritated at Income Tax? Think of it as Tradition," *The Plain Dealer*.
4. Carleton R. Bryant, "GOP staff study finds liability in luxury tax," *The Washington Times*, February 24, 1992, A3.
5. Judith Weber, "Beech Enters Luxury Tax Battle with Negative Statistics for Ammo," *Wichita Business Journal*, June 21, 1991, 7.
6. Al Gore, "Acceptance Speech at Democratic National Convention" (Los Angeles, August 17, 2000), as reported in *The Washington Post*, August 18, 2000, A31.
7. Hadley Cantril, ed., *Public Opinion, 1935–1946* (Princeton, NJ: Princeton University Press, 1951), 377.
8. Richard Nadler, "The Rise of Worker Capitalism," Cato Institute, *Policy Analysis* 359, November 1, 1999, 10.
9. Lesley Mitchell, "Death Often Buries Family Under Mound of Estate Taxes," *Salt Lake Tribune*, May 4, 1997, E1.
10. Travis Research Associates, "Survey of the Impact of the Federal Estate Tax on Family Business Employment Levels in Upstate New York" (Albany: Public Policy Institute of New York State, 1999).
11. Adam Smith, *The Wealth of Nations* (Oxford: Oxford University, 1839), 279.
12. James L. Martin, "Dying Should Not Be A Taxable Event," *Vital Speeches of the Day*, October 1, 1999.
13. Gary Robbins and Aldona Robbins, "Complicating the Federal Tax Code: A Look at the Alternative Minimum Tax (AMT)," Institute for Policy Innovation, *Policy Report Report*, no. 145, March 12, 1998, 3.
14. Robbins and Robbins, "Complicating the Federal Tax Code," 2.
15. Rea S. Hederman, Alison Acosta Fraser, and William W. Beach, "The Triple Whammy of Taxes: How the AMT, Repealing the Bush Tax Cuts, and the Social Security Wage Cap Would Raise Taxes on Millions of Americans," The

Heritage Foundation, *Issues* (February 1, 2007), http://www.heritage.org/Research/Taxes/wm1334.cfm.

16. Nina E. Olson, "We Still Need a Simpler Tax Code," *Wall Street Journal*, April 10, 2009.

17. J. Scott Moody, "The Cost of Complying with the U.S. Federal Income Tax," Tax Foundation, *Background Paper*, no. 35 (November 1, 2001).

18. Malcolm Wallop, "Today's Tax Code Fosters Corruption," in *The I.R.S. v. The People: Time for Real Tax Reform*, eds. Jack Kemp and Ken Blackwell (Washington, D.C.: Heritage Books, 2005), 18.

19. Wallop, "Today's Tax Code," 22–23.

20. Joan Caplin, "6 Mistakes Even the Tax Pros Make," *Money*, March 1998, 104.

21. Brett Fromson and John Mintz, "The Hitch In Taxing the Rich: Higher Rates Don't Worry The Wealthy, Experts Say," *The Washington Post*, November 29, 1992, H1.

22. "Tax Notes," *Wall Street Journal* (March 29, 1995), quoted in Bovard, *Freedom in Chains*, 207.

23. James Bovard, "The I.R.S. vs. You," *The American Spectator*, November 1995.

24. Otis, "A Man's House is His Castle."

25. Bovard, "The I.R.S. vs. You."

26. Rob Wells, "I.R.S. accused of abusing taxpayers as hearing opens," *Associated Press*, September 23, 1997.

27. Office of Sen. William Roth, "Committee to Take Unprecedented Look at the I.R.S." Congressional Press Releases, Federal Document Clearing House, Inc., September 11, 1997.

28. John Picton, "You Think Our Tax Collector is Tough? Try Uncle Sam," *Toronto Star*, March 29, 1992.

29. Ibid.

30. Ecenbarger, "Many Unhappy Returns."

31. Adam Smith, *The Wealth of Nations*, 338.

32. Montesquieu, *Spirit of Laws*, 261.

33. Blackstone, *Commentaries*, 307.

34. Picton, "You Think our Tax Collector is Tough?"

35. Ibid.

36. Ibid.

37. David Cay Johnston, "Investigations Uncover Little Harassment by I.R.S." *The New York Times*, August 15, 2000, A1.

38. Otis, "A Man's House is His Castle."

39. "Roth Statement at I.R.S. Oversight Hearing," Congressional Press Releases, February 2, 2000.

40. Julie Hyman, "Pete Sepp; I.R.S. Now Deserves a C- Grade, Activist Says," *The Washington Times*, April 10, 2000, D2.

41. Johnston, "Investigations Uncover Little Harassment by I.R.S."

42. Albert B. Crenshaw and Stephen Barr, "Is it Really an All-New, Improved I.R.S.?" *The Sacramento Bee*, April 16, 2000, I1.

43. Johnston, "Investigations Uncover Little Harassment by I.R.S."

44. John Kelshaw, "I.R.S. Reform a Fiasco," *Asbury Park Press*, April 28, 2000, A18.

NINE. **Taxing Virtue**

1. 2004 Envy, v. Electronic document, http://www.mw.com/cgibin/dictionary ?book=Dictionary&va=envy&x=10&y=11.
2. "For Better or For Worse: Marriage and the Federal Income Tax," (Washington, DC: Congressional Budget Office, 1997).
3. Jerry Weller, "Q: Is the GOP plan to remove the marriage penalty a good one?" *Insight*, June 8, 1998, 24.
4. James Alm and Leslie A. Whittington, "Does the Income Tax Affect Marital Decisions?" *National Tax Journal* 48, no. 4 (December 1995): 565–72.
5. David Popenoe and Barbara Dafoe Whitehead, "Should We Live Together? What Young Adults Need to Know about Cohabitation before Marriage," The National Marriage Project (January 1999): 3.
6. Richard W. Stevenson, "For Marriage Tax, A Messy Divorce," *The New York Times*, June 7, 1998, 3.
7. Robyn Blumner, "The Marriage Tax," *The Women's Freedom Network Newsletter* 4, no. 4 (Fall 1997).
8. David L. Sjoquist and Mary Beth Walker, "The Marriage Tax and the Rate and Timing of Marriage," *National Tax Journal* 48, no. 48 (December 1995): 547–58.
9. Constituent Letter to Family Research Council, June 1, 2000.
10. Leslie A. Whittington and James Alm, "'Till Death or Taxes Do Us Part," *The Journal of Human Resources* (Spring 1997).
11. Jonathan Weisman, "For Marriage Taxes, an Uneasy Union; Congress would end the $1,400 'penalty,'" *The Baltimore Sun*, June 3, 1998, 1A.
12. John Crouch, "Model Divorce Reform Act," http://patriot.net/crouch/act/index.html.
13. James Alm and Leslie A. Whittington, "The Rise and Fall and Rise . . . of the Marriage Tax," *National Tax Journal* 49, no. 49 (December 1995).
14. Susie Dutcher, testimony before U.S. Senate Finance Committee, April 22, 1998.
15. Bartlett, "Debt Not Rising Precipitously."
16. Stephen W. Hines, *I Remember Laura: America's favorite storyteller as remembered by her family, friends, and neighbors* (Nashville: Thomas Nelson Publishers, 1994), 102.

TEN. **Where Taxpayer's Money Goes: The Answer Nobody**

1. Richard Vedder, Lowell Galloway, and Christopher Frenze, "Taxes and Deficits: New Evidence," Joint Economic Committee (October 30, 1991), quoted in Daniel J. Mitchell, "How a Value Added Tax Would Harm the U.S. Economy," The Heritage Foundation, *Backgrounder*, no. 940 (May 11, 1993): 4.
2. *Source:* http://www.heritage.org/research/features/budgetchartbook/fed-rev-spend-2008-boc-S8-Mandatory-Spending-Has-Increased.html.
3. *Source:* http://www.heritage.org/research/features/budgetchartbook/fed-rev-spend-2008-boc-S10-Mandatory-Spending-per-Household.html.
4. Martin Crutsinger, "First Government Audit Completed," *Associated Press*, March 30, 1998.
5. James Glassman, "No-Account Government," *Washington Post*, April 21, 1998, A21.

6. Ibid.
7. Editorial, "What the GAO Found – or Didn't Find," *Washington Times*, April 3, 1998, A18.
8. Ibid.
9. Ibid.
10. Crutsinger, "First Government Audit Completed."
11. Ibid.
12. Brian M. Riedl and Alison Acosta Fraser, "Fulfilling Your Budget Reform Promise of a Net Spending Cut: A Memo to President-elect Obama", The Heritage Foundation no. 10, December 16, 2008, 4.
13. "Federal Grants-in-Aid to State and Local Governments: 1990-2008," www.census.gov/compendia/statab/tables/09s0414.pdf.
14. Quoted in Ronald D. Utt, "How Congressional Earmarks and Pork-Barrel Spending Undermine State and Local Decisionmaking," The Heritage Foundation, *Backgrounder*, no. 1266 (April 2, 1999): 1.
15. H.L. Mencken, *On Politics: A Carnival of Buncombe* (Baltimore, MD: Johns Hopkins University Press, 2006), 331.
16. U.S. Census Bureau, *Federal Aid to States for Fiscal Year: 1999* (Washington, DC: Government Printing Office, 2000), ix.
17. Ibid.
18. Ibid.
19. Scott Hodge, "The Federal Budget: How to Get Spending Under Control," The Heritage Foundation, Agenda 99, Nov. 11, 1999.

ELEVEN. **Gradual and Silent Encroachments**
1. U.S. Constitution, art. I, sec. 8.
2. James Madison, *The Federalist* No. 41.
3. Quoted in Stephen Moore, "The Unconstitutional Congress: The GOP Misses the Best Argument for Limiting Government," *Policy Review* (Spring 1995).
4. Ibid.
5. Lawrence W. Reed, *A Lesson from the Past: The Silver Panic of 1893* (Irvington-on-Hudson, NY: The Foundation for Economic Education, Inc, 1993), 45.
6. Paul Studenski and Herman E. Krooss, *Financial History of the United States* (New York: McGraw-Hill Book Co., 1952), 214, quoted in Reed, *A Lesson from the Past*, 45.
7. Reed, *A Lesson from the Past*, 45.
8. Higgs, *Crisis and Leviathan*, 85.
9. Ibid.
10. Ibid., 86
11. Frank Luther Mott, *A History of American Magazines, 1885–1905*, vol. IV (Cambridge: The Belknap Press of Harvard University Press, 1957), 401–16.
12. B.O. Flower, "Emergency Measures Which Would Have Maintained Self-Respecting Manhood," *Arena* 9 (May 1894): 823, quoted in Higgs, *Crisis and Leviathan*, 86.
13. Quoted in William Nelson Black, "The Coxey Crusade and its Meaning: A Menace to Republican Institutions," *Engineering Magazine* 7 (June 1894): 313, as quoted in Higgs, *Crisis and Leviathan*, 86.

14. Ibid., 309.

15. Roswell P. Flower, *State of New York: Public Papers of Roswell P. Flower, Governor, 1893* (Albany, NY: Argus Company Printers, 1894), 346, 451, as quoted in Higgs, *Crisis and Leviathan*, 86.

16. U.S. Congress, *Congressional Record*, Senate, 53rd Cong., 2nd sess., January 18, 1894, 979, as quoted in Higgs, *Crisis and Leviathan*, 86.

17. David Boaz, *Libertarianism: A Primer* (New York: The Free Press, 1997), 206.

18. Higgs, *Crisis and Leviathan*, 123.

19. Randall G. Holcombe. "The Growth of the Federal Government in the 1920s," *The Cato Journal* 16, no. 2 (Fall 1998).

20. William Starr Myers and Walter H. Newton, *The Hoover Administration: A Documented Narrative* (New York: C. Scribner's Sons, 1936), 516, as quoted in Albert U. Romasco, "Herbert Hoover's Policies for Dealing with the Great Depression: The End of the Old Order or the Beginning of the New?" In *The Hoover Presidency: A Reappraisal*, eds., Martin L. Fausold and George T. Mazuzan (Albany, NY: State University of New York Press, 1974), 71.

21. Herbert Hoover, *The New Day: Campaign Speeches of Herbert Hoover* (Palo Alto, CA: Stanford University Press, 1928), 16, as quoted in David B. Burner, "Before the Crash: Hoover's First Eight Months in the Presidency," in *The Hoover Presidency: A Reappraisal*, eds., Martin L. Fausold and George T. Mazuzan (Albany: State University of New York Press, 1974), 52.

22. Lawrence Reed, "Great Myths of the Great Depression," Mackinac Center for Public Policy (2000).

23. Stephen Moore, "The Unconstitutional Congress," The Hoover Institution *Policy Review*, Spring 1995.

24. Ibid.

25. Ibid.

26. Murray Rothbard, "1931 – 'The Tragic Year,'" Ludwig von Mises Institute, http://mises.org/rothbard/agd/chapter10.asp.

27. Paul Johnson, *Modern Times: From the Twenties to the Nineties* (New York: HarperCollins, 1991), 245.

28. Ibid.

29. Ibid.

30. Paul Johnson, *Modern Times: From the Twenties to the Nineties* (New York: HarperCollins, 1991), 245.

31. Ibid.

32. James M. Beck, *Our Wonderland of Bureaucracy: A Study of the Growth of Bureaucracy in the Federal Government, and Its Destructive Effect Upon the Constitution*, (MacMillan, 1932), pp. 69–71.

33. Beck, 75–76.

34. Carl N. Degler, "The Third American Revolution," in *Twentieth-Century America: Recent Interpretations*, ed. Barton J. Bernstein and Allen J. Matusow (New York: Harcourt, Brace & World, Inc., 1969), 267.

35. Quoted in Higgs, *Crisis and Leviathan*, 169.

36. Ibid.

37. Higgs, *Crisis and Leviathan*, 169.

38. Ibid., 171.

39. James F. Byrnes, *All in One Lifetime* (New York: Harper and Brothers, 1958), 70, as quoted in Higgs, *Crisis and Leviathan*, 173.

40. Gary M. Anderson and Robert D. Tollison, "Congressional Influence and Patterns of New Deal Spending, 1933–1939," *Journal of Law & Economics*, vol. XXXIV (April 1991): 162.

41. John Joseph Wallis, "The Birth of the Old Federalism: Financing the New Deal, 1932–1940," *Journal of Economic History* 1, vol. XLIV (March 1984): 147.

42. Page Smith, *Redeeming the Time: A People's History of the 1920s and The New Deal*, vol. 8 (McGraw-Hill Book Company, 1987), 598.

43. Anderson and Tollison, "Congressional Influence and Patters of New Deal Spending," 163.

44. Hughes, *The Governmental Habit*, 143.

45. Ibid., 143.

46. Ibid.

47. Ibid., 144.

48. Page Smith, *Redeeming the Time*, 598.

49. Wallis, "The Birth of the Old Federalism," 142.

50. Anderson and Tollison, "Congressional Influence and Patters of New Deal Spending," 164.

51. Quoted in Page Smith, *Redeeming the Time*, 600.

52. Higgs, *Crisis and Leviathan*, 180.

53. *United States v. Butler*, 1936, 297 U.S. 1

54. *United States v. Butler*

55. Madison, *The Federalist* No. 41.

56. Madison, *The Federalist* No. 45.

57. Charles Murray, *Losing Ground: American Social Policy 1950–1980* (New York: Basic Books, 1984), 17.

58. Martha Derthick, *Policymaking for Social Security* (Washington, DC: Brookings Institution, 1979), 231–232.

59. "Outgoing Social Security Head Assails 'Myths' of System and Says It Favors the Poor," *New York Times*, December 2, 1979.

60. Pat Wechsler, "Will Social Security Be There for You?" *Newsday*, January 14, 1990, quoted in Bovard, *Freedom in Chains*, 232.

61. Edward Samuel Corwin, *Total War and the Constitution: Five Lectures Delivered on the William W. Cook Foundation at the University of MI, March 1946* (New York: Alfred A. Knopf Publishing, 1947), 179, quoted in Higgs, *Crisis and Leviathan*, 233.

62. Boaz, *Libertarianism*, 208.

63. U.S. Congress, "Budget Surpluses, Deficits and Government Spending," Joint Economic Committee (December 1998): 12.

64. Ibid., 13.

65. John A. Andrew III, *Lyndon Johnson and the Great Society* (Chicago: Ivan R. Dee Publisher, 1998), 13.

66. Andrew, *Lyndon Johnson and the Great Society*, 71.

67. Council of Economic Advisers, Annual Report, 1964

68. Quoted in Andrew, *Lyndon Johnson and the Great Society*, 67.

69. Andrew, *Lyndon Johnson and the Great Society*, 70–71.

70. Ibid., 79.
71. Ibid., 83.
72. Hughes, *The Governmental Habit*, 217.
73. Andrew, *Lyndon Johnson and the Great Society*, 104.
74. Ibid., 113.
75. Ibid., 110–12.
76. The Heritage Foundation, email from Katherine Bradley to Leslie Carbone, May 7, 2009.
77. Andrew, *Lyndon Johnson and the Great Society*, 86.
78. Ibid.
79. Ibid., 130.
80. Ibid., 118.
81. Andrew, *Lyndon Johnson and the Great Society*.
82. Ibid.
83. Ibid.
84. Ibid., 196.

TWELVE. **Bail-Out Nation**

1. Dean Stansel, "Ending Corporate Welfare As We Know it," Institute for Policy Innovation, *Insightsf* (March 1999).

THIRTEEN. **The Moral Hazard of Spreading the Wealth**

1. Frederic Bastiat, *The Law* (Irvington-on-Hudson, NY: The Foundation for Economic Education, Inc., 1998), 2–4.
2. Ibid, p. 2.
3. Declaration of Independence, July 4, 1776.
4. Julie Star, "The Real Effects of Welfare Reform," e-mail to President Clinton, September 15, 1997.
5. Eric Schlecht, "$cooping for Schools," *Washington Times*, February 20, 2000.
6. "Government, Rights, Mood," *Public Opinion Online*, March 8, 1996, quoted in Bovard, *Freedom in Chains*, 221.
7. "Poll conducted for the Council for Excellence in Government," *Public Opinion Online*, 1995, quoted in Bovard, *Freedom in Chains*, 225.
8. Keith Halpern, "Citizens to Government: Stop Holding Me Back," *New Democrat* (July–August, 1995): 4.

FOURTEEN. **Principles of Sound Fiscal Reform**

1. Adam Smith, *The Wealth of Nations*, 567.
2. Beck, *Our Wonderland of Bureaucracy*, 208.
3. *Wilson v.New* 243 U.S. at 332 (1917),dissent.

FIFTEEN. **Tax Reform Plans**

1. Quoted in Amity Shlaes, "Discredited: How tax credits block tax cuts," *National Review*, August 9, 1999, 37.
2. Daniel J. Mitchell and William W. Beach, "Taxes: Reforming the System to Make It Simple and Fair," in *Issues 2000: The Candidate's Briefing Book*, ed. Stuart M. Butler and Kim R. Holmes (Washington, DC: The Heritage Foundation, 2002), 40.

3. Quoted in James K. Glassman, "Praise the Capital Gains Cut and Pass the Flat Tax," *The Washington Post*, November 30, 1994.

4. Moore, *Cato Handbook for Congress*.

5. David R. Burton and Dan R. Mastromarco, "Emancipating American from the Income Tax: How a National Sales Tax Would Work," Cato Institute, *Policy Analysis*, no. 272 (April 15, 1997): 4.

6. Jeffrey A. Singer, "A Citizen's Guide to the Flat Tax: What it Does, How it Works," Citizens for a Sound Economy Foundation, 12.

7. Mitchell, "How a Value Added Tax Would Harm the U.S. Economy," 7.

8. Paul V. Teplitz, *Value-Added Taxation in Canada and Japan* (Washington, DC: National Retail Institute, 1993), ES-2.

9. Karl Borden, "Dismantling the Pyramid: The Why and How of Privatizing Social Security," The Cato Institute, *Social Security Paper*, no. 1 (August 14, 1995): 5.

10. Milton Friedman, "Speaking the Truth about Social Security Reform," The Cato Institute, *Briefing Paper*, no. 45 (April 12, 1999).

11. David C. John, "Social Security: Improving Retirement Income," in *Issues 2000: The Candidate's Briefing Book*, ed. Stuart M. Butler and Kim R. Holmes (Washington, DC: The Heritage Foundation, 2002), 17.

12. Peter Ferrera, "Putting Social Security in Your Hands," Institute for Policy Innovation, *Insights* (March 1999): 2.

13. Robbins and Robbins, "The Case for Burying the Estate Tax," 19.

14. Stephen Moore, "Fundamental Tax Reform," 72.

15. Ibid., 65.

16. Mitchell and Beach "Taxes: Reforming the System to Make It Simple and Fair," 39.

SELECTED BIBLIOGRAPHY

Adams, Charles. *Those Dirty Rotten Taxes: The Tax Revolts that Built America.* New York: The Free Press, 1998.

———. *For Good and Evil: The Impact of Taxes on the Course of Civilization.* Lanham, Maryland: Madison Books, 1993.

Alm, James, and Leslie A. Whittington, "Does the Income Tax Affect Marital Decisions?" *National Tax Journal* 48, no. 4 (December 1995): 565–572.

———. "The Rise and Fall and Rise . . . of the Marriage Tax." *National Tax Journal* 49, no. 4 (December 1995).

———. "'Till Death or Taxes Do Us Part." *The Journal of Human Resources* (Spring 1997).

Anderson, Gary M., and Robert D. Tollison. "Congressional Influence and Patters of New Deal Spending, 1933–1939." *Journal of Law & Economics* XXXIV (April 1991).

Andrew III, John A. *Lyndon Johnson and the Great Society.* Chicago: Ivan R. Dee Publisher, 1998.

Aristotle, *The Politics.*

Bailyn, Bernard. *The Origins of American Politics.* New York: Vintage Books, 1970.

Bartlett, Bruce. "Debt Not Rising Precipitously." National Center for Policy Analysis (January 17, 2000) http://www.ncpa.org/oped/bartlett/jan1700.html, accessed November 27, 2004.

Bastiat, Frederic. *The Law.* Irvington-on-Hudson: The Foundation for Economic Education, Inc., 1998.

Beach, William W., and Gareth E. Davis. "Social Security's Rate of Return." The Heritage Foundation. *A Report of the Heritage Center for Data Analysis*, no. 98–01 (January 15, 1998).

Bernstein, Barton J., and Allen J. Matusow, eds. *Twentieth-Century America: Recent Interpretations.* Harcourt, Brace & World, Inc., 1969.

Blackstone, William. *Commentaries on the Laws of England, 1765–1769*, vol. 1 Chicago: University of Chicago Press, 1979.

Borden, Karl. "Dismantling the Pyramid: The Why and How of Privatizing Social Security," Cato Institute. *Social Security Policy*, no. 1 (August 14, 1995).

Bovard, James. *Freedom in Chains: the Rise of the State and the Demise of the Citizen.* New York: St. Martin's Press, 1999.

————. "The I.R.S. vs. You." *The American Spectator* (November 1995).

Brown, E. Cary. "Fiscal Policy in the 'Thirties: A Reappraisal." *American Economic Review* 46, no. 5 (December 1956).

Bruun, Erik, and Jay Crosby, eds. *Our Nation's Archive: the History of the United States in Documents*. New York: Black Dog & Levanthal Publishers, 1999.

Burton, David R., and Dan R. Mastromarco. "Emancipating America from the Income Tax: How a National Sales Tax Would Work." Cato Institute. *Cato Policy Analysis*, no. 272 (April 15, 1997).

Declaration of Independence, July 4, 1776.

Fausold, Martin L. and George T. Mazuzan, eds. *The Hoover Presidency: A Reappraisal*. Albany: State University of New York Press, 1974.

"For Better or For Worse: Marriage and the Federal Income Tax," (Washington, DC: Congressional Budget Office, 1997).

Friedman, Milton. "Speaking the Truth about Social Security Reform." Cato Institute. *Briefing Paper*, no. 45 (April 12, 1999).

Harvey Robert P., and Jerry Tempalski. "The Individual AMT: Why it Matters." *National Tax Journal* (September 1997).

Higgs, Robert. *Crisis and Leviathan: Critical Episodes in the Growth of American Government*. Oxford: Oxford University Press, 1987.

Hughes, Jonathan R.T. *The Governmental Habit: Economic Controls from Colonial Times to the Present*. New York: Basic Books, 1977.

Johnson, Paul. *Modern Times: From the Twenties to the Nineties*. New York: HarperCollins, 1991.

Joint Economic Committee, U.S. Congress. "Budget Surpluses, Deficits, and Government Spending." Budget of the United States Government (December 1998).

Journals of the Continental Congress, 1774–1789. Cont. Cong., October 14, 1774, 64.

Kemp, Jack, and Ken Blackwell, eds. *The I.R.S. v. The People: Time for Real Tax Reform*. Washington, D.C.: The Heritage Foundation, 1999.

Kennedy, John F. Speech to Economic Club of New York. December 14, 1962.

Kessler, Charles R., ed. *The Federalist Papers*. New York: Signet Classics, 2003.

Knowlton v. Moore 178 U.S. 41, 109 (1899).

Leff, Mark. *The Limits of Symbolic Reform: The New Deal and Taxation, 1933–1939*. London and New York: Cambridge University Press, 1984, 290–91.

Mitchell, Daniel J. "The Historical Lessons of Lower Tax Rates," The Heritage Foundation. *Backgrounder*, no. 1086 (July 19, 1996).

————. "How a Value Added Tax Would Harm the U.S. Economy." The Heritage Foundation. *Backgrounder*, no. 940 (May 11, 1993).

————. "Why Congress Should Repeal the Tax Code." The Heritage Foundation. *Memorandum*, no. 513 (March 11, 1998).

————. "Time To Sunset The Tax Code." The Heritage Foundation. *Memorandum*, no. 645 (January 28, 2000).

————, and William W. Beach. "Taxes: Reforming the System to Make It Simple and Fair." In *Issues 2000: The Candidate's Briefing Book*, ed. Stuart M. Butler and Kim R. Holmes. Washington, DC: The Heritage Foundation, 2002.

Montesquieu, Charles de Secondat. *The Spirit of the Laws*, vol. 1. Cambridge: Cambridge University Press, 1989, 266.

Moore, Stephen. "The Unconstitutional Congress: The GOP Misses the Best Argument for Limiting Government." *Policy Review* (Spring 1995).

Moore, Stephen, and Dean Stansel. *Ending Corporate Welfare As We Know It.* Washington, DC: Cato Institute, 1995.

Murray, Charles. *Losing Ground: American Social Policy 1950–1980.* New York: Basic Books, 1984.

Olasky, Marvin. *Fighting for Liberty and Virtue: Political and Culture Wars in Eighteenth-Century America.* Wheaton, IL: Crossway Books, 1995.

Paul, Arnold M. *Conservative Crisis and the Rule of Law: Attitudes of Bar and Bench, 1877–1895.* New York: Harper & Row, 1969.

*Pollock v. Farmers' Loan & Trust Co. et. Al.*May 20, 1895.

Popenoe, David, and Barbara Dafoe Whitehead. "Should We Live Together? What Young Adults Need to Know about Cohabitation before Marriage." The National Marriage Project (January 1999).

Reed, Lawrence. *Great Myths of the Great Depression.* Mackinac Center for Public Policy (2000).

———. *A Lesson from the Past: The Silver Panic of 1893.* Irvington-on-Hudson, NY: The Foundation for Economic Education, Inc, 1993.

Reid, John Phillip. *Constitutional History of the American Revolution: The Authority to Tax.* Madison, WI: University of Wisconsin Press, 1987.

Robbins, Gary, and Aldona Robbins. "The Case for Burying the Estate Tax." Institute for Policy Innovation. *Policy Report*, no. 150 (March 15, 1999).

———. "A Tax Deduction for Payroll Taxes: An Analysis of the Ashcroft Proposal." Institute for Policy Innovation. *Policy Reports*, no. 142 (June 1997).

———. "Reducing the Marriage Penalty: A Good Way to Cut Taxes?" Institute for Policy Innovation. *Issue Brief* (July 15, 1998).

Robertson, A. Haeworth. *The Coming Revolution in Social Security.* Reston, VA: Reston Publishing Company, 1981.

Rosenman, Samuel I., ed. *The Public Papers and Addresses of Franklin D. Roosevelt.* New York: Harper & Brothers, 1950.

Shlaes, Amity. *The Greedy Hand: How Taxes Drive Americans Crazy and What to Do about It.* New York: Random House, 1999.

Shughart, William F. II, ed. *Taxing Choice: The Predatory Politics of Fiscal Discrimination.* Oakland, CA: The Independent Institute, 1997.

Slaughter, Thomas P. *The Whiskey Rebellion: Frontier Epilogue to the American Revolution.* Oxford University Press, 1986.

Singer, Jeffrey A. "A Citizen's Guide to the Flat Tax: What it Does, How it Works," Citizens for a Sound Economy Foundation, 12.

Smith, Page. *Redeeming the Time: A People's History of the 1920s and The New Deal.* Vol. 8. New York: McGraw-Hill Book Company, 1987.

Thompson, J.M. *The French Revolution.* Stroud, UK: Sutton Publishing, 2002.

U.S. Census Bureau. *Federal Aid to States for Fiscal Year: 1999.* Washington, DC: Government Printing Office, 2000.

U.S. Constitution.

U.S. v. Carlton, 512 U.S. 26, 33 (1994).

Utt, Ronald D. "How Congressional Earmarks and Pork-Barrel Spending Undermine State and Local Decisionmaking." The Heritage Foundation. *Backgrounder*, no. 1266 (April 2, 1999).

————, and Daniel J. Hickey. "How Government Wastes Your Money: Report Number. 3." The Heritage Foundation. *F.Y.I.*, no. 123 (October 15, 1996).

Wallis, John Joseph. "The Birth of the Old Federalism: Financing the New Deal, 1932–1940." *Journal of Economic History* 1. Vol. XLIV (March 1984).

Witte, John F. *The Politics and Development of the Federal Income Tax*. London: The University of Wisconsin Press, Ltd., 1986.

INDEX

ABOUT THE AUTHOR

Leslie Carbone is a writer living in Virginia. Her work has appeared in magazines including *The Weekly Standard* and *The American Enterprise*, in newspapers from *The Philadelphia Inquirer* to *The San Francisco Chronicle*, and on Web sites like BreakPoint and National Review Online. She has appeared on more than 200 radio and television talk shows, been quoted in national newspapers including *The Wall Street Journal* and *USA Today*, and lectured at more than 100 campuses across the United States and in Canada, including Northwestern University, UCLA, and Cornell University. Ms. Carbone has served as Chief-of-Staff to the late Assemblyman Gil Ferguson of California, Executive Director of Accuracy In Academia, Director of Family Tax Policy at Family Research Council, and Speechwriter for U.S. Secretary of Labor Elaine L. Chao.